THINK
BIG

THINK BIG

*Unleashing Your Potential
For Excellence*

Ben Carson, M.D.
with Cecil Murphey

Legacy Communications Group, Inc.
Franklin, Tennessee

*To all those individuals behind the scenes
who make it possible for me to practice neurosurgery
and still remain socially active.*

To shake the tree
Of life itself and bring down fruit
unheard-of!

—E. A. Robinson

Contents

Part Two:
You Can Give Your Best and Think Big

Introduction

> *The renown that riches or beauty confer*
> *is fleeting and frail; mental excellence*
> *is a splendid and lasting possession.*
> *—Sallust (86–34 B.C.)*

This is a book about giving our best and especially about doing whatever we can to help others—about Thinking Big—one of the important concepts of my life. It might also be called a book about excellence. Or about dedication.

It is also a book about people who give their best and who Think Big.

I chose this theme because our society tends to focus on super-entertainers, sports figures, politicians, or the highly publicized individuals who do outstanding work and get recognized for their achievements. I am all for achievement, and just as much in favor of recognition. But what about those who give their best but never receive recognition? Or financial reward? Or honor? Or fame?

My life has been a rich one, having been blessed by God in many ways. My first book, *Gifted Hands,* * has brought me much recognition and has focused the spotlight on me. Consequently, many people have expressed appreciation for what I have been trying to do.

High school students have written to tell me that the book has challenged them and changed their lives; dedicated teachers have given out copies to all their students; a number of congregations

---

* *Gifted Hands* by Ben Carson with Cecil Murphey (co-published by Review & Herald, Hagerstown, MD, and Zondervan Publishing House, Grand Rapids, MI) 1990.

bought copies of *Gifted Hands* to give to students; I know of at least two businessmen who each bought more than a thousand copies to distribute. And I am grateful.

I am pleased to know that my story has encouraged many and thankful for every word of appreciation, but I also want to point out one of the great truths of life: I did not do it *alone*. I had help along the way.

Competent, committed individuals gave me their best without reservation. Often I receive the recognition, but now I want to pause long enough to shine the spotlight on them, if only for a moment. They deserve it.

Without repeating most of the experiences detailed in *Gifted Hands,* I want to acknowledge the significant individuals who helped Ben Carson climb from the academic bottom of his fifth grade class to become, at age thirty-three, head of pediatric neurosurgery at Johns Hopkins Hospital. One of the youngest persons ever to have such a position, I am the only black person to have such a position at a world-renowned institution. God endowed me with ability, but I would never have been cognizant of those gifts, or used them if others had not taken time to share their talents by giving their best to me.

I hope that now you will walk another step further with me. I want to take you through my life again and tell you about those *special, rare, and gifted* people who have made my achievements possible. And who did it *often without realizing it,* simply by giving their best.

Part One

Giving Their Best
and Thinking Big

There are loyal hearts, there are spirits brave,
There are souls that are pure and true;
Then give the world the best you have,
And the best will come back to you.
                                        —Madeline Bridges

One

Do It Better!

> *It is chiefly through books that we enjoy*
> *intercourse with superior minds. In the best*
> *books, great men talk to us, give us their*
> *most precious thoughts, and pour their*
> *souls into ours. God be thanked for books.*
> *They are the voices of the distant and the*
> *dead, and make us heirs of the spiritual life*
> *of past ages. Books are true levelers. They*
> *give to all who will faithfully use them, the*
> *society, the spiritual presence, of the best*
> *and greatest of our race.*
> *—William Ellery Channing*

Benjamin, is this your report card?" my mother asked as she
picked up the folded white card from the table.

"Uh, yeah," I said, trying to sound casual. Too ashamed to
hand it to her, I had dropped it on the table, hoping that she
wouldn't notice until after I went to bed.

It was the first report card I had received from Higgins
Elementary School since we had moved back from Boston to
Detroit, only a few months earlier.

I had been in the fifth grade not even two weeks before everyone considered me the dumbest kid in the class and frequently
made jokes about me. Before long I too began to feel as though I
really was the most stupid kid in fifth grade. Despite Mother's
frequently saying, "You're smart, Bennie. You can do anything you
want to do," I did not believe her.

No one else in school thought I was smart, either.

13

Now, as Mother examined my report card, she asked, "What's this grade in reading?" (Her tone of voice told me that I was in trouble.) Although I was embarrassed, I did not think too much about it. Mother knew that I wasn't doing well in math, but she did not know I was doing so poorly in every subject.

While she slowly read my report card, reading everything one word at a time, I hurried into my room and started to get ready for bed. A few minutes later, Mother came into my bedroom.

"Benjamin," she said, "are these your grades?" She held the card in front of me as if I hadn't seen it before.

"Oh, yeah, but you know, it doesn't mean much."

"No, that's not true, Bennie. It means a lot."

"Just a report card."

"But it's more than that."

Knowing I was in for it now, I prepared to listen, yet I was not all that interested. I did not like school very much and there was no reason why I should. Inasmuch as I was the dumbest kid in the class, what did I have to look forward to? The others laughed at me and made jokes about me every day.

"Education is the only way you're ever going to escape poverty," she said. "It's the only way you're ever going to get ahead in life and be successful. Do you understand that?"

"Yes, Mother," I mumbled.

"If you keep on getting these kinds of grades you're going to spend the rest of your life on skid row, or at best sweeping floors in a factory. That's not the kind of life that I want for you. That's not the kind of life that God wants for you."

I hung my head, genuinely ashamed. My mother had been raising me and my older brother, Curtis, by herself. Having only a third-grade education herself, she knew the value of what she did not have. Daily she drummed into Curtis and me that we had to do our best in school.

"You're just not living up to your potential," she said. "I've got two mighty smart boys and I know they can do better."

I *had* done my best—at least I had when I first started at Higgins Elementary School. How could I do much when I did not understand anything going on in our class?

In Boston we had attended a parochial school, but I hadn't learned much because of a teacher who seemed more interested in talking to another female teacher than in teaching us. Possibly, this teacher was not solely to blame—perhaps I wasn't emotionally able to learn much. My parents had separated just before we went to Boston, when I was eight years old. I loved both my mother and father and went through considerable trauma over their separating. For months afterward, I kept thinking that my parents would get back together, that my daddy would come home again the way he used to, and that we could be the same old family again—but he never came back. Consequently, we moved to Boston and lived with Aunt Jean and Uncle William Avery in a tenement building for two years until Mother had saved enough money to bring us back to Detroit.

Mother kept shaking the report card at me as she sat on the side of my bed. "You have to work harder. You have to use that good brain that God gave you, Bennie. Do you understand that?"

"Yes, Mother." Each time she paused, I would dutifully say those words.

"I work among rich people, people who are educated," she said. "I watch how they act, and I know they can do anything they want to do. And so can you." She put her arm on my shoulder. "Bennie, you can do anything they can do—only you can do it better!"

Mother had said those words before. Often. At the time, they did not mean much to me. Why should they? I really believed that I was the dumbest kid in fifth grade, but of course, I never told her that.

"I just don't know what to do about you boys," she said. "I'm going to talk to God about you and Curtis." She paused, stared into space, then said (more to herself than to me), "I need the Lord's guidance on what to do. You just can't bring in any more report cards like this."

As far as I was concerned, the report card matter was over.

The next day was like the previous ones—just another bad day in school, another day of being laughed at because I did not get a single problem right in arithmetic and couldn't get any words right on the spelling test. As soon as I came home from school, I changed into play clothes and ran outside. Most of the boys my age played softball, or the game I liked best, "Tip the Top."

We played Tip the Top by placing a bottle cap on one of the sidewalk cracks. Then taking a ball—any kind that bounced—we'd stand on a line and take turns throwing the ball at the bottle top, trying to flip it over. Whoever succeeded got two points. If anyone actually moved the cap more than a few inches, he won five points. Ten points came if he flipped it into the air and it landed on the other side.

When it grew dark or we got tired, Curtis and I would finally go inside and watch TV. The set stayed on until we went to bed. Because Mother worked long hours, she was never home until just before we went to bed. Sometimes I would awaken when I heard her unlocking the door.

Two evenings after the incident with the report card, Mother came home about an hour before our bedtime. Curtis and I were sprawled out, watching TV. She walked across the room, snapped off the set, and faced both of us. "Boys," she said, "you're wasting too much of your time in front of that television. You don't get an education from staring at television all the time."

Before either of us could make a protest, she told us that she had been praying for wisdom. "The Lord's told me what to do," she said. "So from now on, you will not watch television, except for two preselected programs each week."

"Just *two* programs?" I could hardly believe she would say such a terrible thing. "That's not—"

"And *only* after you've done your homework. Furthermore, you don't play outside after school, either, until you've done all your homework."

"Everybody else plays outside right after school," I said, unable to think of anything except how bad it would be if I couldn't play with my friends. "I won't have any friends if I stay in the house all the time—"

"That may be," Mother said, "but everybody else is not going to be as successful as you are—"

"But, Mother—"

"This is what we're going to do. I asked God for wisdom, and this is the answer I got."

I tried to offer several other arguments, but Mother was firm. I glanced at Curtis, expecting him to speak up, but he did not say anything. He lay on the floor, staring at his feet.

"Don't worry about everybody else. The whole world is full of 'everybody else,' you know that? But only a few make a significant achievement."

The loss of TV and play time was bad enough. I got up off the floor, feeling as if everything was against me. Mother wasn't going to let me play with my friends, and there would be no more television—almost none, anyway. She was stopping me from having any fun in life.

"And that isn't all," she said. "Come back, Bennie."

I turned around, wondering what else there could be.

"In addition," she said, "to doing your homework, you have to read two books from the library each week. Every single week."

"Two books? Two?" Even though I was in fifth grade, I had never read a whole book in my life.

"Yes, two. When you finish reading them, you must write me a book report just like you do at school. You're not living up to your potential, so I'm going to see that you do."

Usually Curtis, who was two years older, was the more rebellious. But this time he seemed to grasp the wisdom of what Mother said. He did not say one word.

She stared at Curtis. "You understand?"

He nodded.

"Bennie, is it clear?"

"Yes, Mother." I agreed to do what Mother told me—it wouldn't have occurred to me not to obey—but I did not like it. Mother was being unfair and demanding more of us than other parents did.

The following day was Thursday. After school, Curtis and I walked to the local branch of the library. I did not like it much, but then I had not spent that much time in any library.

We both wandered around a little in the children's section, not having any idea about how to select books or which books we wanted to check out.

The librarian came over to us and asked if she could help. We explained that both of us wanted to check out two books.

"What kind of books would you like to read?" the librarian asked.

"Animals," I said after thinking about it. "Something about animals."

"I'm sure we have several that you'd like." She led me over to a section of books. She left me and guided Curtis to another section of the room. I flipped through the row of books until I found two that looked easy enough for me to read. One of them, *Chip, the Dam Builder*—about a beaver—was the first one I had ever checked out. As soon as I got home, I started to read it. It was the first book I ever read all the way through even though it took me two nights. Reluctantly I admitted afterward to Mother that I really had liked reading about Chip.

Within a month I could find my way around the children's section like someone who had gone there all his life. By then the library staff knew Curtis and me and the kind of books we chose. They often made suggestions. "Here's a delightful book about a squirrel," I remember one of them telling me.

As she told me part of the story, I tried to appear indifferent, but as soon as she handed it to me, I opened the book and started to read.

Best of all, we became favorites of the librarians. When new books came in that they thought either of us would enjoy, they held them for us. Soon I became fascinated as I realized that the library had so many books—and about so many different subjects.

After the book about the beaver, I chose others about animals—all types of animals. I read every animal story I could get my hands on. I read books about wolves, wild dogs, several about squirrels, and a variety of animals that lived in other countries. Once I had gone through the animal books, I started reading about plants, then minerals, and finally rocks.

My reading books about rocks was the first time the information ever became practical to me. We lived near the railroad tracks, and when Curtis and I took the route to school that crossed by the tracks, I began paying attention to the crushed rock that I noticed between the ties.

As I continued to read more about rocks, I would walk along the tracks, searching for different kinds of stones, and then see if I could identify them.

Often I would take a book with me to make sure that I had labeled each stone correctly.

"Agate," I said as I threw the stone. Curtis got tired of my picking up stones and identifying them, but I did not care because I kept finding new stones all the time. Soon it became my favorite game to walk along the tracks and identify the varieties of stones.

Although I did not realize it, within a very short period of time, I was actually becoming an expert on rocks.

The world of books is the most remarkable creation of man; nothing else that he builds ever lasts. Monuments fall; nations perish; civilizations grow old and die out. After an era of darkness, new races build others; but in the world of books are volumes that live on still as young and fresh as the day they were written, still telling men's hearts of the hearts of men centuries dead.

—Clarence Day

Two things happened in the second half of fifth grade that convinced me of the importance of reading books.

First, our teacher, Mrs. Williamson, had a spelling bee every Friday afternoon. We'd go through all the words we'd had so far that year. Sometimes she also called out words that we were supposed to have learned in fourth grade. Without fail, I always went down on the first word.

One Friday, though, Bobby Farmer, whom everyone acknowledged as the smartest kid in our class, had to spell "agriculture" as his final word. As soon as the teacher pronounced his word, I thought, *I can spell that word.* Just the day before, I had learned it from reading one of my library books. I spelled it under my breath, and it was just the way Bobby spelled it.

If I can spell "agriculture," I'll bet I can learn to spell any other word in the world. I'll bet I can learn to spell better than Bobby Farmer.

Just that single word, "agriculture," was enough to give me hope.

The following week, a second thing happened that forever

changed my life. When Mr. Jaeck, the science teacher, was teaching us about volcanoes, he held up an object that looked like a piece of black, glass-like rock. "Does anybody know what this is? What does it have to do with volcanoes?"

Immediately, because of my reading, I recognized the stone. I waited, but none of my classmates raised their hands. I thought, *This is strange. Not even the smart kids are raising their hands.* I raised my hand.

"Yes, Benjamin," he said.

I heard snickers around me. The other kids probably thought it was a joke, or that I was going to say something stupid.

"Obsidian," I said.

"That's right!" He tried not to look startled, but it was obvious he hadn't expected me to give the correct answer.

"That's obsidian," I said, "and it's formed by the supercooling of lava when it hits the water." Once I had their attention and realized I knew information no other student had learned, I began to tell them everything I knew about the subject of obsidian, lava, lava flow, supercooling, and compacting of the elements.

When I finally paused, a voice behind me whispered, "Is that Bennie Carson?"

"You're absolutely correct," Mr. Jaeck said and he smiled at me. If he had announced that I'd won a million-dollar lottery, I couldn't have been more pleased and excited.

"Benjamin, that's absolutely, absolutely right," he repeated with enthusiasm in his voice. He turned to the others and said, "That is wonderful! Class, this is a tremendous piece of information Benjamin has just given us. I'm very proud to hear him say this."

For a few moments, I tasted the thrill of achievement. I recall thinking, *Wow, look at them. They're all looking at me with admiration. Me, the dummy! The one everybody thinks is stupid. They're looking at me to see if this is really me speaking.*

Maybe, though, it was I who was the most astonished one in

the class. Although I had been reading two books a week because Mother told me to, I had not realized how much knowledge I was accumulating. True, I had learned to enjoy reading, but until then I hadn't realized how it connected with my schoolwork. That day—for the first time—I realized that Mother had been right. Reading is the way out of ignorance, and the road to achievement. I did not have to be the class dummy anymore.

For the next few days, I felt like a hero at school. The jokes about me stopped. The kids started to listen to me. *I'm starting to have fun with this stuff.*

As my grades improved in every subject, I asked myself, "Ben, is there any reason you can't be the smartest kid in the class? If you can learn about obsidian, you can learn about social studies and geography and math and science and everything."

That single moment of triumph pushed me to want to read more. From then on, it was as though I could not read enough books. Whenever anyone looked for me after school, they could usually find me in my bedroom—curled up, reading a library book—for a long time, the only thing I wanted to do. I had stopped caring about the TV programs I was missing; I no longer cared about playing Tip the Top or baseball anymore. I just wanted to read.

In a year and a half—by the middle of sixth grade—I had moved to the top of the class. Unfortunately, I had not been content just to read and to learn. I also felt I had to let everyone else in the world know how brilliant I had become. At the time, I honestly believed that I knew more than any of the other kids in my classroom. I thought I was brilliant; actually, I was quite obnoxious.

This important fact did not start getting through to me until I was in the ninth grade. One day I asked one of my classmates, who had never treated me well no matter how hard I tried to be friendly, "Why are you so hostile? Why do you hate me?"

"Because you're obnoxious," he said. "Because you know so much and you want to make sure everybody knows it."

I don't know if I answered or just walked away, but I never forgot his words. In fifth grade, everyone had laughed at me when I did not know anything; now they hated me because I acted as if I knew everything.

Until that moment, because knowledge was new and wonderful and exciting, I thought everybody wanted to hear about everything new that I learned. I had not realized how overbearing I had become. My classmate's cutting words made me aware of how wrong I had been.

The remark did not cure me, but it did force me to admit that I needed to change my attitude. And I did—slowly. Unfortunately, it took a few more experiences before the message really got through.

Once I became known as Ben Carson, the brightest student in his class, I spouted off answers at every opportunity. More than just answers, when any subject came up, I started telling an individual or a group more than anybody ever wanted to know about the topic.

As I later realized, part of the issue involved getting back at those who had laughed at me in fifth grade. They had called me stupid and dumb, but I kept proving again and again that they were wrong. By then they were convinced, but I kept on. It was immature of me and mistaken, but that's what I did anyway.

The boy who never got any answers right on a test in math had totally reversed everything by the time he took advanced algebra. We had a midterm test and the teacher added two extra-credit questions. When she passed back the exams, I saw that one of the smartest boys in the class had made a 91. After class I went up to him and asked, "Hi, what did you make on the test?"

"I made 91."

Momentarily I waited for him to ask, "What did you get?"

When he did not ask, I volunteered, "I got 110—everything right and the two bonus questions too."

"Oh, yeah. That so?" he said and started to walk off.

"Well, maybe you'll do better next time," I said.

"Yeah," he answered without turning around.

"If you need any help, let me know!"

He did not acknowledge that he had heard me.

❖　❖　❖　❖

By eleventh grade I had gotten so caught up in achievement-just-for-achievement's sake that it must have been awful for others to be around me. Then, in one of my chemistry exams, I made only a 99, which was an A—but two others got a 100. No one said anything to me, but I was sure that those other two must have been gloating. They had bettered my grade, which no one had done for at least four years.

Somehow I had convinced myself that I had to be the best and brightest student in the entire high school. When someone did something better—and it was inevitable that it had to happen at least part of the time—it made me think that I was not the best, after all. And if I were not the best, then as far as I was concerned, I had failed.

I really blew that test, I told myself over and over. *If I had just studied a little harder, or maybe taken a little more time in thinking through the answers, I would have made 100.* For the rest of the day, I felt like a terrible, terrible failure. Too vividly I remembered fifth grade and the way some of the kids had treated me.

"I'll never fail again," I promised myself, still not having figured out that so much of this revolved around my attitude.

Then an incident occurred that did more than get my attention: It made me see myself the way others were seeing me.

In the eleventh grade, our entire class took a field trip to the

Detroit Historical Museum. At one point, we were examining pictures of Detroit in 1890. Standing next to Anthony Flowers, I whispered, "Wouldn't it have been great to live back there in those days and to know as much as I know now, because then I could be smarter than anybody else?"

"But you're already smarter than everybody else," Anthony said, "so why would you want to do that?"

"Just for fun," I said. But to myself I asked, *Why* would *I want to do that? Why do I have to prove that I am smarter than anyone else?*

Anthony's simple question forced me to take an intense look at Benjamin Carson. It was a moment of clear revelation when I realized how apparent it must be to everybody that I was always trying to be the smartest person in the crowd. They did not appreciate the constant information that I tried to give them. None of them seemed to like me any better when they discovered that I was smart—in fact, maybe some liked me less.

Then another thought hit me: *Maybe that's not the way I should be. What if I try to be confident in what I'm doing and not make it so obvious that I have to be the best? If I know all of this and use it, isn't that what counts? Who said that I have to push all this information on everybody?*

From then on I did change, because I perceived my need to be different.

In retrospect, as I analyze the intellectual monster I had become to a degree, it evolved because I felt pushed. Mother kept reminding me, saying nearly every day something like, "You should be the best." That idea had become ingrained in me. Yet, she had not intended for me to boast or feel smarter, nor had she meant that I was to haul out my knowledge and display it ad nauseam.

It took a long time to overcome that need to be better than everybody else. Finally, I grasped that Mother had been trying to get me to understand simply that I had to do my best—just my best—and that my doing my best was all she wanted or that anyone could expect. She even said those very words many times, but it still took a long time for it all to come together.

The best turn of events that helped me get all this in perspective came about when I entered Yale University. Until then I had honestly believed that I was smarter than anyone else. Then I met other students (some in the genius category) who had been at the top of their class in high school, who had much wider knowledge than I, and who knew how to study in-depth. I felt outclassed.

Being around those talented students forced me to make significant readjustments in my thinking about my ability. For a few weeks I experienced the emotions of fifth grade all over again. I did intensive soul-searching and praying. This introspection made me realize that I was smart, yes, but not smarter than everybody else. There was no reason that I should expect to be smarter than everybody else. If I were going to achieve goals, I was going to have to work for them just as everybody else does. I was not an innate genius.

Maybe that is the best lesson I learned in my first semester at Yale, because if I had gone to a less-demanding school and continued to sail along on the top, I am sure I would never have attained the subsequent achievements in my life.

One other factor played an important role in my development. I had always had a terrible temper, striking out at anyone who opposed me. One afternoon when I was fourteen, I argued with a friend named Bob. Pulling out a camping knife, I lunged at my friend. The steel blade struck his metal belt buckle and snapped.

Realizing that I could have killed my friend, I raced home, locked myself in the bathroom, and sat on the edge of the tub— my heart filled with shame and remorse over what I had done. I prayed for God to take away my temper.

At one point I slipped out of the bathroom long enough to grab a Bible, open it, and begin to read Proverbs. The verse that struck me the most powerfully was, "Better a patient man than a warrior, a man who controls his temper than one who takes a city" (16:32).

During the two or three hours that I remained in the bathroom, God performed a miracle in my life—He took away my temper, and I can honestly say I have never been troubled with anger since.

I recount this story because that day was the beginning of a lifelong habit—the daily reading of Proverbs. From that day on I have read from Proverbs almost every day. For a long time I did not pay much attention to the verses relating to pride, but those verses, like the constant admonitions from my mother, would eventually sink in.

Words from Proverbs finally got through to me and forced me to rethink much of life. Especially I recall 29:23: "A man's pride brings him low, but a man of lowly spirit gains honor."

The more I read from Proverbs, the more I began to learn how God hates pride and arrogance. The more I read about pride, the more I understood that the Lord was not going to be pleased with me if I continued to be arrogant. "I hate pride and arrogance, evil behavior and perverse speech" (8:13).

Being set free from arrogance did not come overnight, but it began that day. From then on, whenever I got an indication from someone that I was being arrogant, it would feel like a sharp jab in my stomach.

Even now, winning against pride is a struggle. Whenever a person does anything extremely well and others recognize it, it will be a struggle. For me it is worse, because family members of patients frequently say kind things such as, "Oh, you're fantastic! You're great," when we have successful surgeries, and keep repeating, "You're wonderful. You're so gifted." I know that they mean well, but I also know that I do not have a successful surgery without the help of numerous other gifted people backing me up. Moreover, I know that if God had not given me the ability to be a neurosurgeon, I could not accomplish such successes.

As are most people, I am uncomfortable with praise. It is embarrassing to be the subject of a string of complimentary remarks. I have achieved successes—and expect to achieve considerably more—but remind myself that I could not have accomplished anything without the help of an excellent support staff and top-quality colleagues who helped with the preoperative diagnosis and planning. I had to have superb people tending to the critically ill patients during postoperative periods.

There is plenty of credit to go around, especially to the Lord, who had to have arranged the circumstances and given all of us the abilities to do our work.

In reviewing the past few years at Johns Hopkins, I have been the primary surgeon, one member of a *team* that has perfected hemispherectomies.* In late 1987—along with *sixty-nine* others—I achieved a first in medical history by successfully separating Siamese twins joined at the back of the head—successful because both boys survived. Remembering those others, it is easy for me to remember when people start pouring on the praise, that it is not just I who should receive the credit.

Through the years, I have come to realize that God has given me not only the natural gifts of a surgeon but also the sensitivity to feel the hurt of my patients. This, however, does not give me the right to boast—I am only using the gifts that were given to me.

Knowing this does make me thankful.

❖　❖　❖　❖

---

* Hemispherectomy: We remove half of the brain of patients to cure their intractable seizures.

So many times when I was growing up, Mother was standing beside me, saying, "Bennie, you can be anything you want. Just ask God for help. God will help you if you'll help yourself by giving your best."

Or she had told me about the rich and the high achievers and said, "Bennie, you can do anything they can do—only you can do it better!"

All of the many lessons my mother taught me I can combine into this maxim: *Always give your best.*

In pondering that simple advice to always give one's best, I have realized that it is one of the secrets of how I have come from a nearly illiterate, black inner-city neighborhood to a place of prominence. Moreover, I want to keep stressing that I never did it by myself.

In the following chapters, I want to tell you not only how I myself have tried to give my best—to Think Big—but also about others who, in giving their best, have changed lives.

Two

My Mother, Sonya Carson

A mother is not a person to lean on, but a
person to make leaning unnecessary.
—Dorothy Canfield Fisher

G*ifted Hands* really isn't about Ben Carson." A woman said that to Cec Murphey, my co-author, after she had finished reading the book. "It's a book about a mother and her influence. Even in the chapters where she's not mentioned, she is still there—present in everything Ben does."

That woman's perception may be correct. Certainly anyone who knows me or has read anything about me knows that my mother's personality had a strong impact on my life. Because this is a book about Thinking Big and giving our best to help others, I want to tell you about my mother's influence in my early years.

In this chapter, Sonya Carson speaks for herself, using her own words to tell about raising my brother and me.

Sonya Carson:

My own life starts out like the end of a romantic novel. At age thirteen, with practically no schooling, I married a handsome man who promised to make my life happy and exciting. Until then, my life had not been happy or exciting. Although I remember almost nothing about my own parents, I do vividly remember moving from one foster home to another and being ignored or laughed at for being different from the others.

To this day I don't know how many children were in our family. I have heard that there were twenty-four, but I don't remember for sure. Besides myself, I personally know thirteen of them—certainly a lot.

As a child, I did not have friends, not even among my siblings. From as far back as I can remember, I felt different, I was different —and they let me know it. I was chubby, and my hair had a reddish tint. I couldn't talk plainly, and they laughed at the way I pronounced words. I wanted to belong, but I never did fit in.

Then I met the man who would take me away from all of the pain and poverty: Robert Carson, the minister of a small church, who seemed to be everything I wanted in life. In the beginning at least, I think I worshiped him more than I did God. At the time, I did not know much about Christianity, so he had to teach me everything. I went to church, did everything he told me, and tried to act like everyone else.

If I worshiped my husband, he treated me almost the same way. "This is my little china doll," he would say when he intro-duced me. It was not so much of an exaggeration, because that's exactly how he treated me. I had lost my childhood fat, and found that being a little different made me stand out. The day would come when I began to wonder if he had married me just to put me on display. For years I let him treat me like the fragile creature he saw me as. Mr. Carson constantly bought me new clothes and tried to make life nicer and easier for me. When I'd protest about the money he spent, he would say, "I love buying jewelry and minks and anything else that shows off my beautiful little china doll."

After we had been married five years, I finally asked, "Why don't we have children?"

"Children?" He laughed. "Baby, we don't need children!"

"Sure we do," I said. "When people get married, that's one of the things they do. They raise a family." The first few times I brought up the topic of children, he brushed aside the idea. But I was persistent.

During one of the times that I brought up the subject, he said, "You don't need children. You don't need to mess up your beautiful figure by having children. We can have lots of fun without children."

"I don't worry about my figure, and I want children."

"You've got me," he said. "I'm all you need. And you're all I need."

His answers struck me as strange, because most men seem to want children. It would be at least ten more years before I figured out why he acted the way he did.

In the meantime we lived comfortably, maybe even luxuriously. He loved to party and came up with every kind of excuse to go to one. Often we started on Thursday night and did not stop until the early hours of Sunday morning. Many Sunday mornings he had to drink hot sauce to wake him up after a party. That was the only way he could be ready to stand in the pulpit two hours later.

Not knowing any differently, I went with my husband to church on Sunday and the midweek services. Beyond that, I remember little else besides the endless number of parties. As far as the fun times went, I did not care much for them, but, trying to be the good wife, I went with him.

Not having gone to church often as a child, I did not understand much of what went on, so I watched the older women (most of them old enough to be my mother or grandmother), determined to do whatever they did. They would start singing and, after a few minutes when the music got faster and louder, they got excited. Before long, they'd shout and sway in time to the music.

I did just about everything they did, except join in the shouting (although I don't think anyone noticed). I could never quite figure out what they were shouting about, and I just did not see any reason to do it. (I'm the type of person who needs to have a reason for the way I react, and I couldn't jump and shout just because everyone else did.)

Sometimes, however, I felt guilty and condemned myself because I couldn't respond in the way they did. *Is it because they know the Bible and can read it, and I can't?* I wondered. *Are they just better Christians?* I did not know the answers, and I never had any close friends in the church that I could ask.

The longer I stayed around the church, the more I saw of how it operated.

Mr. Carson and other ministers belonged to some kind of ministerial association and spent a lot of time together. Once, when we attended a convention, one of the other preachers started talking to Mr. Carson and me. He was a man they called "hip" because he was tall, handsome, wore the best clothes, and had the kind of voice people like to listen to. "I'd like to have your wife be my secretary," he told my husband.

"Sure." Mr. Carson grinned, as if the man's offer was the best news he had heard in five years.

"Hey, look," I said as I laughed, "I hardly know how to spell my own name, much less be a secretary."

"Oh, I know you'll do just fine," the other preacher said, and he kept smiling at me.

"Why would you choose me to be your secretary?" I asked. "I wouldn't know how to make a complete sentence." I expected my husband to object, but he did not.

"Listen, Sonya, you're a smart little woman."

"Not that smart."

"I can teach you what you don't know."

My husband kept grinning, making me know he liked the idea.

Since my husband approved, I said, "I still don't understand all of this, but I guess I'll become your secretary."

After the morning meeting finished, he said, "Come with me, Sonya, and we'll get started." We left, and he took me to his motel room.

"Come on, sit down," he said, indicating a corner of the bed.

Ignoring the bed, I sat in a chair and whipped out a notepad and pencil from my purse, because I knew that's how secretaries behave. I waited, wondering what I was supposed to do next.

"Put that aside," he said, motioning to the notepad and pencil. "We don't need that right now."

Before I could reply, a knock at the door interrupted us. He opened the door, and a waiter walked into the room, carrying a large tray with two glasses and a bottle of champagne that was being chilled in an ice bucket. As soon as he tipped the waiter, who then left us, the preacher opened the bottle and started to pour two glasses full. "Let's drink champagne."

"Thanks a lot," I said, "but I would rather get along with the matter of the work you want me to do." I had a tough enough time trying to pretend to enjoy the parties with my husband, and did not want to start partying with this man. Already I could feel myself getting irritated with him. He just did not seem very serious or businesslike, but then I reminded myself that he was a minister, a man of God. I did not say anything more.

I heard him opening the champagne and pouring it. "Come on, Sonya. Join me for a drink." He walked over to me and held out a glass.

I shook my head. "I'm ready to work—"

"Don't worry about that," he said, taking the pad from my hand and tossing it on the floor. "We're going to hop into bed."

For a few seconds I stared at him, waiting for the words to sink in. "We're what?"

He repeated his words.

"You're asking me to hop into bed with you? And you're a minister?" I was so naïve that such an idea had not occurred to me. Naïve, yes, but I wasn't stupid, and I told him so. "You get yourself another bird because this bird don't fly that way."

"That's no way to talk," he said as he stepped toward me.

"If you move any closer to me, I'm going to yell that you're bothering me. If I start yelling, they'll hear me screaming for two city blocks."

Obviously he had not expected that kind of response. He stepped backward and stared at me, a confused look on his face. "Okay, okay," he said. "Don't yell. Look, it won't go any further; just act like it did not happen, and you needn't come back any more. Just don't let anybody know this happened."

I picked up my pad and walked out of the room.

Once we got back to the convention, the preacher ignored me. He even went out of his way to say to people (when he knew I could hear him), "Ignore Sonya. That girl doesn't know what's going on." He wanted them to think I was stupid and not worth being friendly toward. From then on, through the rest of the convention, the other women shunned me. Although I felt hurt by their treatment and a little lonely, I did not say anything—after all, I'd received much harsher treatment in foster homes.

That terrible experience opened my eyes. I continued to go to church, attend the parties, and still did everything my husband asked me to, but it had no reality for me, even though I did not know how to put it into words then. It was just a big game.

My life with Robert Carson just rocked on after that. Even though I still did not ask many questions, I watched everything that was going on. I did not know much about Christianity, but the people that I dealt with did not seem to fit with what little I did know.

❖   ❖   ❖   ❖

I still wanted to become a housewife and a mother. Until we married, I had worked hard, no matter where I lived. I'd always done what I could to help out the family, but when we got married, that wasn't the way Mr. Carson wanted it.

"You take care of yourself now," he would say. "I promised I would look out for you and take good care of you, did I not?" He even hired a woman to come in every week and clean our house. When I protested, he had his standard answer, "I can't have my little china doll getting all tired out, can I?"

To him, that was a reason. For me, it was boredom. I had nothing to do and no friends. When we married, my husband introduced me to a lot of people. Even though I knew the names of hundreds of people, I never felt I belonged. Just as in childhood, I did not fit.

I often thought that if we had children—a real family—I'd belong to somebody. I'd have a husband and children to love me, and we could be comfortable together. I kept at my husband until he finally agreed to have children. Curtis was born in 1949, and then two years later, Ben.

From the time of Curtis's birth, the next eight or nine years was the happiest time in my life—the only happy time, really. I loved my boys, and I felt fulfilled. Now I had a purpose in being alive.

For a long time I had not been happy with Mr. Carson. It was more than the parties and the heavy drinking. One thing that bothered me most was that he was a spendthrift. He had plenty of money coming in but got rid of it almost as soon as it touched his hands.

For instance, he often went to downtown Detroit. While there, if he saw something he wanted me to have, he would buy it, regardless of the price. One time he bought a necklace that cost eight hundred dollars—a great deal of money even in those days. As far as I know, I was the only woman in our neighborhood who had a mink coat, something I did not particularly want anyway.

In fact, I did not want any of the fancy clothes or the jewelry. For me, having a home, two sons, and a husband was enough, and if Mr. Carson would change his ways, I kept telling myself, it would be a perfect life.

For three or four years after Ben was born, my husband seemed to be settling down. He loved the boys and played with them just like any normal father. Besides being a preacher, my husband worked at one of the Cadillac plants.

How the children loved their daddy. By the time Ben was three or four, on most afternoons, he had started asking me, "Is it time for Daddy to come home?"

"Not yet," I'd have to say.

When it got close to four o'clock, and we could expect Mr. Carson to return, I'd say, "Almost time now." Ben would run outside, sit on the porch, and wait. His father usually took the bus and walked down the alley to the house. As soon as Ben saw him, he would race with his arms outstretched toward his father. A minute later, the two of them would come inside, laughing and enjoying just being together.

Unfortunately, my husband's alteration did not last. By the time Curtis entered school, Mr. Carson began to act as if the boys were a hindrance to his life, often not coming home until quite late. He did not have time to play with Curtis and Ben any more. Or he was too tired.

New facts started coming to light about my husband. He would get telephone calls that I wouldn't have thought much about if he hadn't whispered, making it obvious that he did not want us to know what was going on.

From time to time, his sister would call and talk to me. She was angry with him. As the words spewed out, she would let little hints drop. She never accused him, but she made it obvious that she knew what he was doing. Although I did not want it to be true, I soon had to face the facts: He had plenty of money because he was dealing in illegal whiskey. Though I can't say for sure, he may have been dealing in dope. I do know that he had more money around than he could possibly have made from his preaching and factory job—and he quickly spent it all.

Then one day I found out a big secret that shattered my life. I don't want to go into detail, except to say that I learned that Mr. Carson had another wife and children. He had married years before we met and never divorced her. I couldn't believe it. I did not want to believe it—yet I knew it was true.

I confronted my husband who, after a number of denials, did admit that he had another family. When I asked more questions about them, he lied so much that I stopped asking him.

What should I do now? I kept asking myself that question for a couple of weeks. We had two wonderful boys. Their welfare had to come first.

I decided that I would just make the best of the situation. Curtis was seven, Ben was five, and these boys *need their father,* I decided—for their sake, I can't leave. Besides, I had no idea where to go or what to do or how I could support myself.

So, I tried to continue living as I had before, but each day the situation seemed to get worse. Mr. Carson was home less and less often, and when he did come home there were more whispered conversations on the telephone.

I never spoke against their father to the boys. And I did not know anyone to talk to about my situation. I did not have any friends; I even stopped going to the church where my husband preached.

About that time I started having physical problems and my nerves seemed constantly on edge. Then I started having trouble sleeping—some nights I did not get more than one or two hours of sleep. Eventually I went to a doctor who gave me medication, but I still did not sleep properly. The pressure got so intense that I knew I had to do something.

On one visit, my doctor said, "Mrs. Carson, you have to talk to me. Tell me what's wrong."

"I told you. I just can't sleep. The medicine—"

"Your problem isn't physical. It's much deeper."

"Some family problems. Your husband?"

"Yes." I did not say much, but I did mention that our marriage wasn't going well. "My husband isn't around much and he wastes all his money," I added.

"You need to talk to a psychologist," he said.

"I couldn't do that."

"You want to get better? You want help?"

When I did not answer, he made an appointment for me. I went to the psychologist.

An insightful man, the psychologist said, "It's quite obvious that you have some deep-seated problems. You need to tell somebody. It's good to talk about these things. You can tell me because I don't know any of your neighbors or friends. Nobody else will know, not even your husband."

It wasn't easy, but I did open up. At last I had somebody who wanted to listen to me. I told him what I knew and also my suspicions about my husband's dealing dope.

"You don't have to put up with that," he said. "In fact, you shouldn't. You've got the boys' future to think about."

"I just don't know what to do," I said.

The psychologist, working with my doctor, took over for me then and got the ball rolling. "You can't stay in that situation," both of them advised.

They were right, of course. I couldn't stay any longer, yet I was scared and confused. How could I support myself and two boys? I needed somebody to advise me. The doctor and psychologist sent me to an attorney who thought the whole thing should be talked over with Mr. Carson. If he would cooperate, they could clear up everything easily, the lawyer supposed.

But my husband refused to cooperate. Again the two doctors suggested I leave. "Otherwise," the medical doctor said, "we'll just keep filling you full of drugs."

"The pressure won't get any better," said the psychologist.

Even though it was the right thing for me to do and I knew it, I still was uneasy. Packing up and leaving with my two sons was one of the hardest things I've ever done in my life. I phoned my sister, Jean Avery, who lived in Boston, and asked if the boys and I could stay with her until I figured out what to do.

"Of course," Jean said. Her husband, William, was every bit as persistent in urging us to come.

During our two years away from Detroit, Mr. Carson took up with his other wife. She began signing my name to checks and, in a short time, ran through every cent I had managed to put into savings, including the fund I had set up for the boys' schooling.

If I had had doubts about our marriage's surviving, all of them were gone. I made up my mind that I was going through with a divorce. "I'm going to raise two fine boys on my own," I told my sister with more conviction than I really felt.

When I thought more clearly about my decision, I had no idea how I could do it. "Look at me," I said aloud to myself one day. "What can I do? I don't have any education. No work experience. I don't know how to do anything."

Just then a thought came to me as clear as if a voice had said aloud, "Maybe not, but I can learn." And I knew I could.

For the next couple of years I had my ups and downs. Several times the pressure became so great that I couldn't fight any more. When that happened, I had enough sense to know I had to get professional help. I checked into mental hospitals, leaving the boys with my sister. She never told them where I was, only that I had to go away for a few days.

At one point, matters got so bad that I felt that I just couldn't take any more—that nothing was going to work out for me. I was so depressed that I was convinced that nobody cared whether I lived or died. If I died, I reasoned, my boys would be better off in a foster home. Or with Jean and William, who had no children of

their own. I had gotten so dejected—physically and emotionally—
that I did not want to fight any more.

One morning I picked up a half-empty bottle of prescription
sleeping pills and counted them out, one at a time. There were
twenty-four. "That ought to be enough," I said. By taking them, I
could sink into a peaceful sleep and never have to wake up again.

If my sister had not come into the bedroom and found me,
noticed the empty medicine bottle, and immediately called the
hospital, I wouldn't have awakened.

The next day, while I was recovering from having my stomach
pumped, a woman named Mary Thomas came to visit me. She
introduced herself and said, "God loves you."

I stared back at the strange woman. She had the brightest smile
I'd ever seen. "Jesus Christ died for you."

"Don't tell me about God," I said. My throat hurt to talk
because of the tube that the doctor had put through to my stomach,
but I managed to say, "I don't want to hear that stuff. God's just as
much a fake as anything else. I don't need any part of that."

"God does love you," she said again quietly. Again she smiled
so brightly, that I couldn't doubt her sincerity.

I ignored Mary Thomas, but she did not go away. She stayed
right beside my bed. In her soft voice, she kept telling me that
God had not given up on me and never would.

"You want to talk?" I finally asked. "Then tell me about
something else. We might really be able to hit on the same bases
on some other topic—but not anything about God. God is no
good. I know that because I was married to a minister."

"I don't know about your husband, but I do know about
God," she said.

Quietly, Mary Thomas talked about God and quoted several
Bible verses. She was different, I had to admit, from any Christians
I had met before. No matter how angry I felt or how rudely I
reacted, she never argued with me or allowed me to upset her.

Mary continued to visit me. Slowly it began to sink in that she cared about me. She would talk about God. Sometimes Mary opened her large Bible and read a few verses. Once, she handed me the Bible, "Here, read it for yourself."

I shook my head, "I can't read much."

"Then I'll help you. You just try." As I tried to read, she prompted me, helping me sound out the hard words and telling me the proper names.

Before I left the hospital, she gave me a Bible. "This is for you, Sonya," she said.

"For me? But why?"

"I want you to have it. It's a gift."

As I took it, I was surprised that she would care enough to give me a Bible. It seemed like such a special gift.

"I hope you'll read it."

I did not answer. I think I would have cried if I had tried to speak. Right then I decided that I would learn to read the Bible. *If anybody else can read,* I thought, *I can, too.*

Then another thought came to me: *If anybody else can do it, I can do it better.* I did not worry about whether this was true, but it changed my attitude. *I can do whatever I make up my mind to do.* That awareness produced in me an iron will. From that time on, I decided that I could learn to do anything that anybody else could do.

That powerful thought became so important that I couldn't forget about it. I said to my sons again and again as they were growing up, "Boys, if anybody else can do it, you can do it better."

I believed it and I wanted them to believe it, too.

❖ ❖ ❖ ❖

Jean and William Avery had become Seventh-day Adventists, so it seemed natural for me to go to the church where they went. I heard more and more about a God who loves us and about Jesus

Christ who died for us. As I slowly learned to read the Bible, just as slowly I began to believe.

The day came when I faced another low point. Suicidal thoughts troubled me once again. Yet I kept remembering what the pastor had said. "There is a God—a God who cares. This God can do great things for you." He had said so many more things, but that much I remembered.

"God, You've got to help me," I said. "I don't even know if I'm praying properly, but I know I need Your help."

Nothing had changed drastically, but I knew that God had heard me—it was an inner certainty that God was with me and would help.

One day I said, "Lord, if You can take nothing and make a world out of it, You can take my situation and make it work—for the boys' sake. I don't care so much about myself, but my boys need help. They deserve a chance."

From then on, God did do remarkable things in my life. I would pray for guidance and afterward would know what to do—there was not so much a voice as a certainty, a feeling of what to say or do. Every day, again and again, I prayed that God would help me say and do the right things to motivate my sons and not discourage them. I did not want to force them into anything, only to love them into wanting to do what is right.

I found work right away even though it did not pay much. I did not have trouble with getting jobs because I was willing to do anything. I worked hard, too, developing a philosophy that I was going to do the best job that anybody could ever do. When I mopped a floor, I wouldn't quit until it was the cleanest and shiniest floor ever seen.

None of my jobs paid much, but I did not worry about it. I

was working, and I was managing to take care of my boys.

About that time I remember telling God, "I don't have any friends. I don't have anyone else to turn to. God, You're going to have to be my friend, my best friend. And You're going to have to tell me how to do things and give me wisdom, because I don't know what to do." About that time I heard a commercial on television or the radio, that said, "You do your best, we do the rest." That fit the way I felt about God. I was going to give God my best and then it was up to God to do the rest.

I wonder how many times in the next dozen years I prayed, "God, You just have to intervene for me, I'm an empty pitcher in front of a full fountain. You have to fill me. You have to teach me."

In those years I really learned to trust in God, and we became friends and partners.

❖   ❖   ❖   ❖

By working double jobs and saving every penny I could, I finally brought my sons back to Detroit. Both boys had been doing all right in school when we left, but they had regressed badly—partly, of course, because of the separation from their father, having to live in a Boston tenement, and going to school with children who did not seem to have much desire to learn.

"We'll get by," I told them, "because God is going to help us." Fortunately, I knew how to sew, so I kept them in clothes. "They might not be the kind of clothes you want, but at least they're clean."

One day I said to the boys, "We're going to have a family altar." That's how we said it in the Adventist church. It meant that the three of us would pray and read the Bible together. We would do it every morning. It was hard to get the time right, but we did it. A lot of times I had to leave early, before they got out of bed. I'd set the alarm. "Boys, you have to get up after I'm gone. You pray for yourselves and just ask God to guide you and to give you strength. Ask Him to send His holy angels to watch over you and to help you study the best you can."

During all those growing-up years I kept working at two, often three jobs. I knew about public assistance, but did not want to go that route because I'd seen too many mothers just stop trying. At one point we did get food stamps, but only for a few months. I wanted to be independent and pay my own way. According to the divorce decree, Mr. Carson was supposed to support our sons, but he provided very little money. "I'll do my best, Lord," I'd say when I walked out of the house every morning, "now You do the rest."

❖   ❖   ❖   ❖

Ben has told the story about his terrible report card in fifth grade. When I saw how bad the boys' grades were, my heart sank. I couldn't be home to help them. Even if I had been home, I did not know enough to be of any help. As poor a student as he was, by the time he was in fifth grade, Ben could already read better than I could.

During that time, I had been learning to sound out words, and my reading improved. As this happened, reading became important to me, and I knew it could be even more important for my sons because if they became interested in reading, they could actually learn anything they wanted to know.

"God, You're my partner and my friend," I prayed. "I don't know what to do about Curtis and Ben. They're both failing everything. They've got to do better. Most especially, they've got to learn to read." When I was praying, the idea came to me to put them on the book assignment.

"Learn to do your best," I kept telling them, "and God will do the rest. Whatever you choose to do in your life, you can do it. I'm not going to tell you what to choose to be, but I think you can be the president, or a pilot, or the best doctor in the world. You can be the best carpenter in the world. Whatever you make up your mind that you want to do, just do your best."

At times, one boy or the other encountered difficulty and wanted to give up, but I wasn't going to let that happen. "Curtis, you're smart enough to do that lesson. Someone had to think it up, and whoever thought it up knew the answers. You can do the same."

Their grades improved when they started reading two books a week. I did not tell them they had to come home with a report card full of A's, but I did tell them they had to improve in every department. When either boy did not show a marked improvement, I got right on him with all the love and understanding I knew. "By the next report card," I said, "you're going to be doing a lot better."

During fifth grade, Ben's biggest problem was math. As we talked, I realized that he did not know his times tables. "You need to learn them," I said. "Ben, if you learned your times tables, math would be easier for you."

He looked at me with a confused look. Then he held up the book and showed me the printed tables. "Here they are from two to twelve. What do I do with them? There are so many."

"You memorize them."

"All of them? It would take a year!"

"Listen, Ben, it won't take *you* a year. It might take some boys a year, but those boys are only half as smart as you are. You start right now. Just go over them. Two times two is four. Three times two is six. Just keep at them until you know all of them."

"Nobody could memorize all of them."

"Bennie, I did not get beyond third grade, but I know them." I started quoting the nines tables for him.

When he realized I could recite the times tables all the way through twelve, he also knew that I wouldn't let up on him until he learned them.

"Mother, you are the meanest mother in the world, trying to make me learn all this. It's hard work."

"Hard work won't hurt you," I answered. "Besides, I think you're the smartest boy in the world. I think you're going to set a record in learning them." I did not raise my voice—I tried never to raise my voice, yet Bennie knew that the only way to shut me up was for him to learn his times tables.

I worked with him for a while, and he was doing pretty well—but Bennie liked to play. Because he wasn't doing as well as I thought he should, I grounded him. "Okay, you can't go out and play until you learn your times tables. All of them up through your twelves."

He learned them in a hurry.

❖   ❖   ❖   ❖

I don't remember whipping either boy more than once or twice. Because I vividly remembered my own childhood with its regular beatings, I did not want Curtis and Ben to have that kind of memory. If I talk to them enough, I decided, I could help them to do whatever was right and not have to punish them.

"You can do it," I would tell them. "You try now. Let's try and see how well you can do it."

Both boys responded. Sometimes their work wasn't up to my expectations, but they did their best. In those instances I'd say, "The next time you're going to do it better."

At one point the boys wouldn't get both their chores at home and their schoolwork done. One time Curtis said, "Ben did not want me to do my work, so I did not get it done."

"What Ben wants for you isn't important. It's what you want for yourself. Nobody can hinder you from doing what you want, if that's what you set your mind to do. You can always find a hook to hang excuses on, but they're only excuses. You don't have anyone to blame but yourself. Nobody else makes you fail."

A few days after I said those words to Curtis, a man came by the house, selling books. One of them had a poem in it that I liked. I bought the book and memorized the poem, "Yourself to Blame." I quoted it often to the boys because it says what I really believe.

Here's the poem in part:

> If things go bad for you—
> And make you a bit ashamed,
> Often you will find out that
> You have yourself to blame . . .
>
> Swiftly we ran to mischief
> And then the bad luck came.
> Why do we fault others?
> We have ourselves to blame . . .
>
> Whatever happens to us,
> Here are the words we say,
> "Had it not been for so-and-so
> Things wouldn't have gone that way."
>
> And if you are short of friends,
> I'll tell you what to do—
> Make an examination,
> You'll find the fault's in you . . .
>
> You're the captain of your ship,
> So agree with the same—
> If you travel downward,
> You have yourself to blame.*

❖ ❖ ❖ ❖

---

* Mayme White Miller

When Curtis was eleven and Ben was nine, I realized that the boys argued almost every day about who was to wash dishes and who had to dry. Every job around the house they managed to fuss over. When I'd intervene, both boys would get upset at me.

"You always tell us what to do," Ben said. "Like we don't do anything unless you tell us fifty times."

"Yeah," Curtis agreed.

I did not say much then because I did not know how to answer. For the next two days I prayed about what they had said. "God, I need help again," I said. "I need a plan to make them feel responsible for themselves. Give me wisdom so that they won't resent my telling them what to do."

An idea came to me.

That evening, I called the boys to the table and said to Curtis, "I'll tell you what. I know you don't like me to give you boys orders. So we're going to change that. I try to do the best I can in setting up rules around here, but I'm under a lot of pressure. Why, I bet you could write out plans that would work better than mine. Don't you think so?"

Curtis did not ever say much, but he beamed when he realized that I was serious. Then he nodded.

"You write the rules you would like to go by. Put down what you would like to do, and that will be your job. Give yourself so many silver stars for doing it good."

"Okay," he said.

"How about this?" I suggested. "You boys earn blue stars for doing it better than average, and gold stars for doing the best."

"I like that idea," Ben said.

"That's not all," I said. "I've been giving you an allowance. From now on, we'll base your allowances on how well you do your work."

The boys discussed it together and agreed. Curtis started writing out rules. To my surprise, they put down things I wouldn't have

asked them to do. Real hard things. As I remember, here are some
of the rules they wrote:

— We will cut the lawn.
— We will wash the dishes and have the floors clean when
   you come home from work.
— We will fold the clothing. (I did the washing, but they did
   not volunteer to do that.)

They also added the time of day when they would do each of
the jobs. "Now just don't tell us to do it," Curtis said.

"I won't," I said.

They really did what they had promised, but more than that,
they learned to cooperate with each other.

I was so proud of them that after a few weeks I said, "Since
you've done so well, I'll tell you what we're going to do. One week
out of the month, you're going to tell me what to do. The other
three weeks I'll tell you what to do."

It worked beautifully. They were so nice to me that I wanted
them to take over for the other three weeks—but I did not ask
them to. They did chores like cleaning out the refrigerator and
planning the meals. As part of their responsibility, they decided to
make sure that our meals were properly balanced. Maybe they did
not do too good at that part, but they sure tried. However, after a
few more weeks of this arrangement, Ben said, "You know, I liked
it better when you told us what to do."

"How about you, Curtis?" I asked. "Did you like it better that
way?"

He nodded.

"Okay, then you've decided that maybe I'm not such a bad
mother after all."

"You're a good mother," Curtis said.

"The best mother in the world," added Bennie.

After that, we never had any more arguing over who did what.

❖ ❖ ❖ ❖

I believe that if we have something inside our heads, nobody can take it from us. I allowed no excuses for failure. Particularly I wouldn't let my boys use racial prejudice as an excuse. I ran into those attitudes when I was out on the job, but I did not have to accept the things people were saying about black persons or anybody else.

After I got acquainted with God and we entered into partnership, I just knew that God did not make any race or nationality to be inferior or superior. We were black, but that did not mean we were dumb and supposed to fail. God loves everybody and wants only good things for us. I tried to get my sons to grasp that what God does for one, He'll do for anyone else.

I used to tell Ben and Curtis, "I think God made different nationalities to see what our reaction was going to be toward each other. Maybe God made it for a special measurement just to see if we could really love someone who is different from us."

One day while I was reading, I came across this verse in the Bible: "If anyone says, 'I love God,' yet hates his brother, he is a liar. For anyone who does not love his brother, whom he has seen, cannot love God, whom he has not seen. And he has given us this command: Whoever loves God must also love his brother" (1 John 4:20–21).

My boys learned an important lesson that is so simple: *God loves us all, and all of us are equal in God's sight.*

❖ ❖ ❖ ❖

At school, the boys were doing well. We still had a few problems to work out at home. We solved the last big issue when I laid down the rule that if they were going to be late, they had to call me at the places I worked (I made sure they always had the numbers). "That way, all of us know where the others are."

Home was then fine; school was excellent; I did have trouble with my neighbors. They learned about our household rules, and they let me know they did not like the way I was raising my sons.

One woman in particular liked to tell me how to raise my family. When she found out that the boys helped me cook, she said, "You're making sissies out of those boys, and they'll never be anything."

"Say what you want, but my boys are going to be something. They're going to learn to be self-supporting and learn how to love other folks. *And* no matter what they decide to be, they're going to be best in the world at it!" I said and walked away.

At the time, I did not know what the word "sissy" meant, but from the way she said it, I knew it wasn't good. I finally looked the word up in the dictionary.

Of course it hurt me that my neighbors said mean things, but I acted as if I did not care. I had a plan: My boys were going to have a good life because, with God's help, they were going to make their own way.

My job was to prepare them. And I turned to God for help every inch of the way.

Since then, prepared to do God's will, I studied and obtained my GED, went on to junior college* and became an interior decorator specializing in furniture restoration, upholstery, and ceramics.

---

* While in junior college, I taught sewing classes.

Three

Special People in My Life

> *The mind is not a vessel to be filled but a*
> *fire to be ignited.*
>
> *—Plutarch*

There is no such person as a self-made individual. Some might dispute that, but I argue from my own experience. True, I came from a poor, single-parent family, and my mother worked ten to fifteen hours every day to keep us off welfare (although at one time we did have to rely on food stamps). By fifth grade no one challenged my position at the bottom of my class. As we also learned, my eyesight was so poor that I couldn't see the teacher from the back of the room. Until I received an eye examination and glasses, however, I did not know how poor my eyesight was.

My list could go on, but I think I've made my point about my beginnings. As indicated in the previous chapter and in my earlier book, *Gifted Hands,* I have come a long way. *But I did not do it by myself.*

Throughout my life at various times, specific individuals have touched my life and enabled me to climb from the bottom of my class to the top of my profession. I could not have done it without such *special* people.

In this chapter I single out those whom I regard as special people—those unique individuals who saw potential in me long before I perceived it in myself—or who challenged me to do more, even when they did not realize that they were challenging me—the people who helped guide me toward excellence.

First on the list is William Jaeck, my fifth grade science teacher, the man who started me upward. Besides being a genuinely nice guy, he was the first teacher to recognize my intellectual abilities. For as long as I could remember, Mother had been telling me, "Ben, you're a smart boy," but when a teacher said, "That's wonderful" and even pointed out to the class the value of my information, it was the beginning of change for me.

From the moment in his class when I identified the lava-formed obsidian, William Jaeck began to take notice of me. Perhaps he saw a spark of talent for science. Although I am not sure of the reason, he showed an interest in me. Being a fatherless boy who was trying to push up from the bottom of the class, I probably would have responded to anyone who took time to show any interest in me.

Mr. Jaeck, whom I remember as being a big man with an equally large voice that exuded enthusiasm, emphasized the study of nature and animals. To make his classes more meaningful, Mr. Jaeck did not just display pictures—his science room contained a collection of animals. At one time or another I remember seeing an opossum, a weasel, mice, guinea pigs, and a variety of birds. One day he brought in a baby red squirrel that, he said, had been abandoned. Students at Higgins Elementary raised the squirrel (that we named "Maynard").

Several times he took us on field trips. Once we went to a nearby pond so that we could observe the ducks and fish. Another time we examined the trees and flowers at a cemetery. Especially I remember when the entire fifth grade went to a flower show in downtown Detroit.

The change in my relationship with Mr. Jaeck came the day I identified a black, glass-like obsidian stone in class. He not only noticed me and made certain that the rest of the class knew my achievements, but Mr. Jaeck did something else that I will never forget (and for which I will always be thankful!). Before he moved on in his lesson that day, he said, almost casually, "Benjamin, why don't you come by after school? Let's talk about a rock collection."

I am sure that he had no realization of the impact of those words on my life. With his help, I did start a rock collection. Besides, he allowed me to work directly with his animals and fish. (I especially remember playing with his crawfish.)

Every time we talked, he stimulated my interest by teaching me something new or by affirming what I had already learned. Within a short time, Mr. Jaeck allowed me to look through the microscope to see the protozoa and to examine microscopic plants.

Mr. Jaeck, enthusiastic about science, taught the subject in such a way that some of that enthusiasm spilled over onto me. From that time on, I was hooked on science.

Many mentors challenged me to give my best.

Perhaps it is not quite accurate to refer to as mentors those who probably have no idea how deeply and profoundly they affected the direction of my life. Still, that is the most direct statement I can make about those benefactors who were involved in my medical training. Some did this quite instinctively. They were individuals who just naturally gave the best and the most of themselves. Their examples, along with (or sometimes without) their words, stimulated me.

❖ ❖ ❖ ❖

The next special person in my life is Dr. James Taren, a neurosurgeon and one of the deans of the medical school at the University of Michigan. His eloquent explanations in clinical medical presentations about patients and neurological disease processes awed me. Listening to his presentations enamored me with what neurosurgeons can do. Even more, his messages began to make me aware of what I myself could do.

Probably then in his forties, Taren was a relatively thin man, about five-foot-nine, with reddish-brown hair. A neat dresser in the latest cut and fashion, he drove a Jaguar. "Flamboyant" is the one best word I can think of to describe him.

Once during a clinical medicine presentation, he gave as an example a woman with a progressive movement disorder that had rendered her nonfunctional. She continued to deteriorate, so Dr. Taren decided to perform a then-dangerous and controversial stereotactic procedure, which involves a special type of frame and lesion maker that looks like something out of a Frankenstein movie. Nevertheless, it enables a surgeon to work with precision on destructive lesions and certain portions of the brain without disturbing much of the adjacent tissue.

After the presentation, someone said, "But, it was dangerous, wasn't it? The patient might have died."

"Sure, it's a dangerous procedure," he said, "but look at the alternative *if we do nothing.*"

Those words stuck with me. Although at the time I had no idea of their impact, I would remember those words many times when I faced difficult problems. When I first started doing hemispherectomies, more than one parent had to face the fact that if I performed a hemispherectomy, their child could die. In most of those instances, I heard myself echoing Dr. Taren's words, "But look at the alternative if we do nothing."

In each case, the parents always agreed. If we did not try a radical procedure, the child would die anyway.

Although I had known since the age of eight that I wanted to be a doctor, I did not know in which area to specialize. At one time I thought of psychiatry and of other different fields at various times, including being a general practitioner. Once I came under the influence of James Taren, however, the question was settled.

Dr. Taren never urged me to be a neurosurgeon, but he inspired me by his way of working and his presentations. During my last two years of medical school, he was my advisor.

It was not that I felt especially close to him, because I did not. In fact, I was in such awe of him, I felt privileged that he knew my name. He knew of me—as did everyone in neurosurgery—because I had completed two rotations in that area (it's unusual for anyone to do that) and got honors in both.

Because I spent long hours reading about the field, asked questions, had an extensive knowledge of neurosurgery, and kept trying to learn everything I could, Taren and others seemed impressed with me.

Several times their words such as, "Nice work," or "You did fine!" gave me just the uplift I needed.

I list James Taren as a mentor, even though I doubt that he has any idea of how highly I regard him. To me, he embodied the ideal master neurosurgeon—the kind who knows just about everything about neuro-anatomy. Yet by the way he went about his work, I did not feel that he was trying to impress anyone. He was just being who he is.

If he had not chosen to be a neurosurgeon, Taren would still be the man everybody looks up to. Even though I have always been ultraconservative, I still admire this dashing, efficient, and very able man.

Some people simply exude confidence. Taren is one of them. Being around him made me sense that he gives his all to what he does. His manner and attitude make it clear that he expects his students to do likewise. Just by being in his presence, in his lectures, or with him in the operating room, made me want to give my best. That is why I admired Dr. Taren so much then. I still do.

❖ ❖ ❖ ❖

In chronological order, the next special person to me has to be

George Udvarhelyi. When we met, he was head of Johns Hopkins neurosurgery training program. Now a retired professor of neurosurgery, he is the director for cultural affairs for the medical center.

George Udvarhelyi interviewed me for my internship at Johns Hopkins and is the one who got me into the program by recommending me. (I learned later that they selected only two students a year out of an average of one hundred twenty-five applicants.)

From my perspective, George and I began a special relationship almost from the moment I walked into his office at Johns Hopkins. Immediately he put me at ease, perhaps helped by the tasteful decoration of his office, or its atmosphere, which implied that I was sitting down with a man who genuinely wanted to hear what I had to say.

Since that day and even now, the key particular about George is that he is just as interested in the person as he is in the person's disease.

During my internship, when we did rounds, George would wait until we grouped around him before he would ask in his soft Hungarian accent, "Vhat do you know about de patient?"

The first time or two he asked, none of us quite understood his question but we started giving him the diagnosis.

"No, no, not that," he interrupted. He was not asking us about the disease. "Vhat does this man do? Vhat does he do for a living?"

Those questions left a lasting impression on me. The man in the bed isn't "just a patient" but a human being with a name and a life outside the hospital.

This outstanding doctor constantly emphasized the humanitarian aspect of medical care. He wanted to make sure that patients were as comfortable as possible and knew what was going on. He wanted them to have a voice in the decision-making process.

On a number of occasions when he would be talking with the residents, someone would say, "It's time for me to go off," (meaning that he had completed his hours of duty). "Vhat do you mean, it's time for you to go off?" he would reply with a blustery voice.

"Vhat do you mean, you're off? The patient is in trouble. Dere is no off. You haf to take care of de patient. That is most important."

What could any of us say to that? George meant exactly what he said and did not want us to forget it, either. He would launch into a lecture on the spot, time and again, reminding us that we were there for the sick, and that it was not a matter of their treatment fitting into our schedules. "You are here to serve the sick. Do not ever forget that!"

One time, George went on an especially long tirade. The object of the lecture was a resident student who had been on duty and was obviously extremely tired. He folded his arms and nodded a few times as the words continued. Finally the resident brought his clipboard to chest level and then let go. It crashed to the floor.

"I quit," he said. He walked out. (Later he did come back.)

As much as I admired George Udvarhelyi, I knew that he got on the nerves of some residents because he was exacting and allowed for nothing less than our absolute best. For me, that was part of what made him so admirable—he refused to allow us to behave in a slovenly manner in any aspect of patient care.

One thing George Udvarhelyi impressed upon me that I do not ever want to forget is that when I take on the commitment to be the physician for a patient, I am making a commitment of my *total self.* I am not to be the physician only when it is convenient; I can make an unspoken pledge to be there for my patients when they need me.

"Othervise, go be a pathologist," he would say. "Be someone who doesn't deal vitt living things."

I thought then and continue to think that he is absolutely right!

When making rounds, George Udvarhelyi frequently introduced a philosophical aspect. Suddenly in the middle of an examination, he would pause, as if it had just come to him. "Vhat did Aristotle have to say about a situation like this?"

More often than not, we residents stared at our feet or glanced at each other. "Vell, think about it some then." He would say a few words to lead us along. Finally one of us would usually make the connection. If we did not, he would finish off by telling us, although it did not end even then. He would let his eyes search our faces and then ask, "Vell, vhat happens now? Do you agree with Aristotle?" and wait for us to answer.

Obviously George wanted each of us to think deeply about every person who came under our care. For him, good medical treatment was only part of our task. More than any other doctor I have ever met, George Udvarhelyi pushed us not to treat patients as if they are nothing more than a type of disease or ailment.

One time when we were discussing types of seizures and their treatment, he said, "Vell, who did surgery for the first epilepsy seizure? How did he map out the brain?"

The answer: Walter Penfield, a famous neurosurgeon.

"Now then, how did Walter Penfield map out the brain? Vhat did he think about it? Did he think the person possessed a soul?"

When one of us answered, "Yes," he nodded and then asked, "Ah, but how did Penfield come to believe there is a soul?"

He guided our discussion for another ten minutes. At the end, I felt greatly enriched because he made everything a lesson in the historical and philosophical details. No one else talked in this manner. He wanted us to know how great surgeons and thinkers of the past understood disease, and how the state of medicine had evolved over the centuries, particularly in the last hundred years.

For me, George Udvarhelyi's teaching method made him invaluable for my training. Yet not all of the residents responded that way.

"He's a real pain," remarked one of the residents to me, who was hearing any negative statement for the first time.

"Really?" I asked. "I find him fascinating."

"Same-old, same-old," he said. "We have to go through all of this stuff."

"I didn't come here for more lectures," said another resident. "That's why we have classrooms. I just want to get on with it."

Their opinions did not matter to me; he was a valuable teacher and a special mentor-friend who remains a friend today.

❖   ❖   ❖   ❖

Thinking of my medical mentors brings me back to Hopkins and to the man who has been a true mentor in every sense of the word: Donlin Long.

I was a resident at Johns Hopkins from 1978 to 1983. After a year in Australia, I returned to Hopkins in the summer of 1984. Within months after my return, the chief of pediatric neurosurgery left, and through the recommendation of Don Long, I became the new chief of pediatric neurosurgery.

That I was only thirty-three—which in medicine is quite youthful—could easily have been reason enough for me to be rejected for the position. Don Long made it clear to everyone that he believed that I could do the job.

I could write endlessly about Don Long's help along the way but will mention only a few instances.

In *Gifted Hands* I recounted in detail that Don Long, aware of prejudice that might be waiting for me, made it clear and irrevocable that if a patient refused to be treated by me, Johns Hopkins would refuse the patient. He had no time or sympathy with those who saw skin color as a barrier to competence.

He was so comfortable with his lack of prejudice that he kidded Reggie Davis about tokenism. Reggie was the second black person to complete the neurosurgery program at Johns Hopkins. "Reggie, after the job Ben has done here, you don't have a chance of getting into this program."

Then he laughed. Only a man free of prejudice could have

done that.

Don did not help me because of my race, and he certainly did not hinder me because of it. That's the kind of person he is. His support and his strong sense of fairness buoyed my self-confidence.

During my first weeks at Hopkins as an intern, when I first came into contact with Don Long, I realized a simple principle on which he operates. If we know and understand human anatomy and we are reasonably intelligent, he assumes that we can figure out how to do almost anything.

I will always remember something that Dr. Long said when I first met him: "Anyone who can't learn from other people's mistakes simply can't learn, and that's all there is to it. There is value in the wrong way of doing things. The knowledge gained from errors contributes to our knowledge base."

He also insisted that "You must have a sound rationale for what you are doing right now." It did not so much matter what someone else had said for or against a procedure. If we could come up with sound reasoning for what we wanted to do, he encouraged us to believe that it was worth doing, whether someone else approved or not—quite a courageous stand. It was a way of saying, "Learn everything you can, but think for yourselves."

Through the years, I have been involved in several radical (and therefore controversial) procedures. Each time, I have gone to Don and explained what I wanted to do and why. Not once has he ever advised me not to go ahead.

Probably the most significant case (which I detail later in the book) involved a woman pregnant with twins. One of them developed hydrocephalus while still in the womb. I proposed putting a shunt in the affected baby while the baby was still in the womb—a very controversial suggestion. In fact, only a few weeks earlier, the *New England Journal of Medicine* had featured an article speaking against such a procedure.

I explained everything to Don, who knew about the recent

article. When I finished, he said, "It sounds quite reasonable to me. I think it's going to work. You have my blessing to do it."

Actually I did not have any doubt of his support, because I knew that my reasoning was sound. Also, I knew that Don is a man willing to try something new even though everyone else says that it can't be done.

Just before I left his office, Don said, "Ben, whatever we need to do to protect you, medically or legally, we will do it."

I never doubted his word.

Don is incredibly busy and must be a member of half a dozen important committees on neurosurgery, which is quite time-consuming. Additionally, he continues to carry a heavy patient work load. Yet, from the first, he always had time for me. (I don't for a minute believe that it was just for me—he is a man who makes time for *people.*)

While I was still a resident, every time I walked into his office he would put down whatever he was doing—a behavior that I had never observed before and that impressed me tremendously.

"What's on your mind?" he would ask in such a friendly way that it was as if he had said, "Ben, I've got all the time in the world. What do you want to talk about?" Most departmental chairmen are not as congenial as he; I have known a few I would not even describe as being friendly.

From Don I picked up an important principle—one of those lessons I learned by observation and not from any formal or informal lecture:

Be Nice To People
—All People—
Even When You Don't Have To Be.
Everybody Is Important.

"Don Long doesn't have to be nice," I said to a friend recently, "and yet he is. It's his nature to be kind." Of course, people appreciate his warmth. Even when it comes to technical knowledge or operating skill, he is not arrogant. And he is a person who would have every excuse to be.

The incident with the Binder twins probably gives the best indication of this man. In February 1987, in Ulm, West Germany, Theresa Binder gave birth to twin sons. They were Siamese twins joined at the back of their heads, who couldn't learn to move as other infants can. The parents had to learn how to hold their sons in a way that well-supported both of them. Because their heads turned away from each other, Mrs. Binder had to prop them against a cushion and hold a bottle of milk in each hand to feed them.

The twins shared no vital organs, but they did share a section of the skull and skin tissue, and the major vein that drained fluid from the brain and returned it to the heart. No one had recorded a case of successfully separating twins of this type in which both children survived.

When the German physicians contacted us at Hopkins, I studied the available information and talked with several colleagues, notably, Mark Rogers, Craig Dufresne, David Nichols, and especially Donlin Long, the chairman of neurosurgery. If undertaken, the procedure would be more than a one-doctor affair. Tentatively I agreed to the surgery, knowing that it would be risky and demanding. Ultimately, my decision was based on the strong possibility that we could do it. If successful, this surgical separation would give two boys a chance to live normal lives.

Don could have made a number of comments when I presented the case to him. As head of the department, he had the right to take over the case. (This does happen in many places!) He *could* have said, and would have been perfectly within his right to do so: "Because of the seriousness of this situation, I'd better take this case and let you assist me." He could then have gotten all the publicity and accolades. He could have, but then he would not have been Donlin Long.

Whereas some top-ranking individuals I have had to deal with make me feel as if they're listening only until I shut up so that they can have their say, Don is not that way. He has a style of listening so that the speakers have a sense that he hears every word. That is how he listened to my explanation. When I finished, Don smiled. "This is your case, Ben. You figure out how you want to do it, and I'll assist you." This is typical of his character. The head of the department volunteered to assist me in the surgery.

❖ ❖ ❖ ❖

Art Wong holds a special place in my heart, too. When I think of giving one's best, I have to hold him up as one of the best examples I know.

He ranks as one of the top residents I have ever observed going through the program, both when I was a resident and since I have been a faculty member. In our program we have had some incredibly impressive people as residents, who are either number one or close to the top in their medical school class. I still put Art Wong above them all.

Art was a pleasant fellow, eager to learn everything, even as a junior resident. Oriental, he was about five-feet-five inches tall, somewhat stocky, baby-faced, and always seemed to wear an impish little smile.

"Yes, I can do that."

Whenever I think of Art, I can still hear him say those words. He had an air of supreme confidence, yet wasn't being cocky. The man truly believed that he could do just about anything. The fact is, he could! Even as a junior resident, he could do numerous things technically that many of the senior residents had not mastered.

By the time he was chief resident, Art Wong, without any question, was the best. I would have rated him as better in neurosurgery than ninety-nine percent of faculty members around the country. He was superbly gifted. When we worked together, it was obvious to me that Art was well on his way to becoming one of the preeminent neurosurgeons in the world.

What I liked most about Art, though, was that he was fun to be around. Sometimes when we went into the operating room and worked together on a shunt, I would take the belly and he would take the head (or vice versa).

"Shall I do it faster than you?" he would ask as his impish eyes glowed. "I can, you know."

We would race—both of us being careful not to go out of the bounds of safety. Neither of us wasted movements, but he would make light, chattering comments as he worked. In those instances it wasn't unusual for us to be able to do a complete new shunt in fewer than fifteen minutes. For a resident, that is quite unusual. Most of the Hopkins staff knew about Art Wong's technical skills. When I operated on Craig Warnick,* Susan, Craig's wife who is also a nurse at Hopkins, actually asked me, "Would it be all right if Art Wong assists you?"

"Of course," I said, quite pleased that she wanted Art. Whereas I had no hesitation in agreeing, it is rare for somebody in the medical profession to ask for a particular resident to assist. The request reinforced to me how highly everyone regarded him.

Effortlessly, Art Wong endeared himself to others. He gave of himself and did it so warmly and caringly that many of us liked just being around him.

After Art finished his residency, he was still connected to Hopkins. He then went to the Barrow Institute in Arizona for

---

* His story is told extensively in *Gifted Hands,* (pp. 185–200). Craig suffered from Von Hippel-Lindau (VHL). Individuals with this (usually hereditary) rare disease develop multiple brain tumors as well as tumors of the retina.

additional post-residency training as a neurovascular fellow. One day he spoke with me by phone about a paper we were publishing jointly, as he needed a few more details before he put it into what would be its final form.

Two days later I was called to Don Long's office. He closed the door. "Sit down, Ben." From the expression on his face, even though he tried not to let it show, I knew that something was wrong. His chin quivered slightly before he said, "Ben, I have some bad news." I remember staring at him with a hundred possibilities flipping through my mind.

"Art Wong," he said softly. The name seemed to hang in the air before he added, "He drowned yesterday."

"Art? That can't be. He's an excellent swimmer!" I did not want to believe it. Although a part of my brain knew Don was telling me the truth, I couldn't accept it. Not Art Wong, that warm and gifted human being. "There has to be a mistake."

"No mistake, Ben," he said. One of our other residents who was also doing summer research at Barrow had called Don.

Immediately I phoned Dr. Spitzler, the chief of neurosurgery at Barrow. "I've just heard a rumor about Art Wong. It can't be true—"

"I'm afraid it is," he said. He kept talking, but I couldn't take in the rest of the information. Not Art Wong, I kept thinking. *Not that wonderfully happy man.*

Before hanging up, Spitzler did suggest that I call the sheriff for any further details. I took down the number and thanked him. Still numb, I stared at the phone for a long time. I wanted to know what had happened, but I did not want to make the call. To learn what had happened meant that I would have to acknowledge the death of my friend.

After several minutes, I called the sheriff.

"The best we can figure out," he said, "Mr. Wong was swimming and—"

"But he was an excellent swimmer, I know that—"

"Yes, but apparently he did not have experience with whirl-pools." He explained that when people get sucked into a whirlpool, they should not struggle against it. "The idea is to hold your breath long enough for it to deposit you wherever it takes you." He added a few more details and said, "At any rate, that's how we think it happened." He then expressed his sympathy before hanging up.

"It just can't be true," I said as I sat in my office. Yet, I knew it was true, and that I had to face that reality. All my life I had heard people use the expression that "it felt as if someone had just pulled the rug out from under them." That's how I felt. It was as if I now sat on the bare floor and couldn't get up. Silently I kept asking, *God, how can this be? Why would something like that happen?*

I had to be alone for a few minutes to talk to God about Art and my own sense of loss. "Lord, Art was a guy who was just top of the line in everything. What a tremendous loss this is to everybody here. What a tremendous loss to the world. Just a silly, freak accident. How can this be?"

It took me a while to battle through the disbelief. As I began to accept it, the numbness dissolved into a pain that hurt so deeply, I could never find words to describe it. I did not know that it is possible to hurt as keenly as I did at that moment.

After a few minutes, I came out of my office. Within the department, everybody already knew, because Art had endeared himself to all of us. Despite the work load, for the next half hour or so, we all seemed to need to talk to someone about Art.

"Remember that time when . . . ?" I must have heard those words at least ten times. All of us mentioned one way or another what a great guy Art had been.

All of us who had worked with Art were so grief-filled that we canceled everything but emergencies for the rest of the day. It was one time when I just could not be a professional. The pain was too deep. A rare soul, now —

He is a portion of the loveliness
Which once he made more lovely. *

—*Shelley*

❖   ❖   ❖   ❖

Carol James has been at Hopkins for more than twenty years and is one of the most insightful individuals I know. She is very pretty, of medium height, and wears her blonde hair long.

Carol James is one of my three PAs, although she is the senior PA in the entire neurosurgery department. My two other physician assistants in pediatric neurosurgery, Kim Klein and Dana Foer, are relative novices, but they, too, are rapidly coming into their own and doing excellent work. Because they are young, talented, and pretty, some people have begun to refer to them as "Ben's Angels"—a take-off from the old television show, *Charlie's Angels.*

With the exception of my wife and my mother, Carol James knows me better than anybody else in the world. Carol certainly spends more time with me. One of the advantages in working with Carol is that she knows how I think. When I am occupied in the operating room for twelve hours, or I have to be away, or a situation worsens, she knows exactly what to do. She honestly knows how I would react and what I would do in various circumstances.

With regularity, when we're both talking with a patient, for example, we find ourselves talking this way:

Ben: It was probably just a matter of someone's . . . uh . . .

Carol: —not being aware of the family history.

Or as we both walk out of a room together, she might say, "You don't have to say it. I know exactly what you're thinking." A few times I've asked, "Then tell me."

She has always been right—she did know. Now I believe her when she says so.

---

* *Adonais,* Percy Bysshe Shelley

Carol is a people-centered individual, and she spends time with each patient. There is no way that I can spend the same amount of time with everyone, explaining the complex operations, all the ramifications and contingencies, yet Carol will take endless hours sitting down with families, explaining the pros and cons, reassuring them, and answering all their medical questions. She has an intuitive sense of just how to handle each person. Sometimes she draws diagrams, or will bring in dolls to explain, or show them an actual shunt, so that they will understand how a shunt is pumped.

In addition, Carol reads my mail. I trust her to answer most of it because she knows what I would say anyway. Although I read what she dictates for my signature, I rarely have to make a single change. She fields the phone calls that come from referrals and decides whether they are appropriate for us versus someone else to do. She examines the material, reviews the X-rays, then presents all to me with her insights and recommendation.

What would I do without Carol James in the operating room? If I have to step out, she keeps the residents in line and makes sure they don't do anything inappropriate because she knows so thoroughly how I do things. It's gotten to the point (and I love it!) where people who need something from me, go directly to Carol because she is more available. This frees me to do more surgery-related things.

When residents come on pediatric neurosurgery, they sense immediately that Carol knows much more about the area than they do. She gains their respect without difficulty. In fact, Carol handles the residents so well that they love her. For many of them, she functions as a mother, even though she is hardly old enough.

In some ways Carol is also a mentor to the other PAs who come on the scene. For the last couple of years Carol has helped to organize and promote an awareness of physician assistants among the public. She is also heavily involved with conventions and programs.

When I have to write an article, Carol gathers the research material. In 1989, when I had the supervision of five students doing clinical projects, they were really her students; she showed them how to find information in the library and in the medical records department, and directed them to the significant papers and studies relating to their projects.

Basically, Carol's presence allows me to do twice as much as I would ordinarily be able to do. And she does it *without grumbling*. This dedicated person comes in every morning between 7:00 a.m. and 7:30 a.m. She stays every night as long as I stay, however long that is. I seldom leave before 7:00 p.m., and occasionally as late as 11:00 p.m., but she's still on the job. No question about it, I just could not do it without her. I feel blessed to have someone like Carol working with me.

As I have mentioned, I'm a softie and it's easy for people to take advantage of me. Carol, along with Pat Brothers, prevents that from happening. She calls herself the "mean lady," although she's not really mean. Actually, Carol is just more practical than I am, and she recognizes limitations more readily than I do.

To sum up the importance of Carol James: She is one more outstanding example of a person who is dedicated to her job and who unstintingly gives her best.

Four

Parents and Patients

If ye have faith and doubt not, . . . if ye
shall say unto this mountain, Be thou
removed, and be thou cast into the sea; it
shall be done. And all things, whatsoever ye
shall ask in prayer, believing, ye shall
receive.

—KJV

Occasionally I talk with people who see doctors as people who do nothing but give of themselves and never receive from anyone else—especially not from the patients. That is totally false.

The longer I remain in my profession, the more I realize how much I receive from those who come to me for help. Something about the process of sharing and caring not only bonds doctors and patients (as well as the patients' families) but teaches valuable lessons about life just from being in contact with them.

Immediately I think of two different families.

First, the Thomya family from Thailand, whose story is more about the mother than the patient.

A little girl named Bua, who was less than a year old, had a vascular malformation that encompassed most of her brain, going from the back of her head to the front and even into the face and nose. In time, Bua's constant nosebleeds could cause her to bleed to death.

After many attempts at surgery in Thailand failed, in 1987 Tanya Thomya decided to bring her child to the United States.

One of the Thai doctors who had been taking care of Bua had done an anesthesiology rotation at Hopkins and, of course, knew that we did many relatively daring surgeries. Through his contact with Mark Rogers, he helped them arrange to have Bua transferred to Hopkins. Immediately we started to evaluate this tremendous vascular anomaly. We spent some time trying to figure out a way to correct her condition.

Initially I planned to attack it directly. But in the operating room, once I had made a burr hole in the skull, the bleeding was so ferocious that I did not know if I could get it to stop. Finally I did, but in the process it became abundantly clear that I wasn't going to be able to follow my initial plan—she would bleed to death before I could do any corrective work.

Dr. Gerard Debrun, a famous neuro-radiologist in neuro-radiological intervention, had already worked out techniques for blocking and correcting vascular malformations with balloons, glue, and other substances injected into the arteries. Using the results of his pioneer technique, our team mapped out a plan. We would take Bua back to the operating room where I would expose a major portion of this malformation. Then we would inject thrombogenic (clot-inducing) little coils with metal fur on them into the vascular malformation. (The idea was that they would "encourage" the blood platelets to stick to them and form blood clots.) We reasoned that if we could get enough thrombogenic coils into the appropriate part of this vascular malformation, the whole malformation would clot.

For six hours we worked. In the process, we inserted more than one hundred coils. As far as I could tell, the coils had done the job. Bua's nosebleeds stopped.

Mrs. Thomya took her infant daughter back to Thailand. For over a year, Bua did well and was developing normally. Then the nosebleeds started again.

The mother rushed her child back to Hopkins and we examined

little Bua. The horrible vascular monster had come back again, creating new channels of malformed vessels.

"We'll go back in again," I told the worried mother. "We'll do everything we can."

She did not say much, but the obvious relief on her face showed that she was well aware of the seriousness of Bua's relapse. I sensed that she feared I would tell her, "I'm sorry, there's nothing more we can do."

Altogether, we performed four operations on Bua, all of them to tie off portions of the malformation. On the final surgery I got down to the last big channel that had to be tied off. When I went out to see Mrs. Thomya, I said, "We can't be sure, but it looks as if we may win this time."

Mrs. Thomya had patiently stayed at Hopkins around the clock with her daughter, devoting every minute to her child. Despite the weariness etched in her deeply circled dark eyes, she smiled. "Thank you," she whispered.

Following the usual procedure, Bua went into the intensive care unit. Only hours later, Bua had a seizure, followed seconds later by another and then another. She was anoxic (a state of lack of oxygen) for a while.

After the seizures, Bua never rebounded. She lived but since then does little more than lie still and look around. Since a number of us had been involved with Bua, it was one of those sad defeats that depressed us for days.

I decided to tell this story, however, not because of the complexity of the situation or the failure at the end but to focus on Bua's mother. Through the years I have observed many, many dedicated parents, but none quite like Mrs. Thomya. The mother stuck by her child's side throughout this whole ordeal. She gave her best—her all—to that child.

Beyond what we would call the obvious sense of dedication, she had developed an intuitive union with little Bua that I have never seen in any other parent. In a way that none of us ever quite understood, Mrs. Thomya totally knew her daughter. It was as if they had developed an inner, mystical, unspoken communication. For example, with what seemed to those of us here as only a casual glance, she accurately knew when her child was about to vomit, when the child was feeling well, and when she wasn't.

The second time Mrs. Thomya brought her daughter to America, Bua lived in the hospital for six months. Her mother stayed by her bedside, unwilling to leave. "This is my child," she would say firmly. For her, it was the only explanation she needed to offer.

Being from Thailand, they had no insurance. This meant they had to pay the horrendous bill out of their own pocket. The Thomyas had been a wealthy family when Bua's problems started; they were a poor family by the time her treatment ended. Despite this, Mrs. Thomya refused to give up. She and her husband were willing to use all their resources for the sake of this child.

As for dedication, I do not think I have ever seen a less selfish or more attentive mother. She was separated from her husband, her other children, and her big house. No one could have been more devoted to Bua's well-being. She once said of the other children, whom she missed intensely, "They have a father and grandparents. Bua has no one but me. I must stay."

Month after month, whatever was required, Mrs. Thomya did it without the slightest hesitation or complaint.

I felt extremely sorry for the mother and for the family as I saw their resources being depleted. So many times I wished there were something that could be done to help them financially. Although I wrote off as many bills as I could, and the hospital helped with some of the expense, the cost of living in America, the expensive equipment, medicine, and supplies made the total bill astronomical. But again, Mrs. Thomya's love for her child—a child that she knew might not live, or if she did, would be severely retarded— never slackened.

When it looked as if all was going well, I was thrilled; when it looked as though all was not going well, I was devastated. Yet, throughout all the stressful months, Mrs. Thomya remained pleasant and optimistic.

"You can only do your best," she said to me. "That is all God asks of any of us, is it not?"

Even now, Mrs. Thomya stays in touch. In early 1990 she sent us pictures of her new baby. She is going on with her life and giving herself to her family. And Bua is not neglected. Mrs. Thomya will continue to care for her retarded child until Bua dies.

No one could give more than Mrs. Thomya has given.

❖   ❖   ❖   ❖

The second family that comes to mind is the Pylants. Neil and Carol Pylant had wanted a son more than they wanted anything else. Being devout Christians, they prayed faithfully for God to give them a child. Finally the Lord blessed them with a son, whom they named Christopher.

From earliest childhood, Christopher loved stories about Jesus and other biblical heroes. As soon as he was able to string words together into sentences, Christopher started quoting Bible verses from memory. This almost sounds like a fictional story of the perfect family, but it was not like that for long. Tragedy struck.

When Christopher was four, he began to weave and stumble. Then his parents noticed other abnormal behavior such as his difficulty in handling his secretions, almost to the point of foaming at the mouth. Then the child developed double vision.

When first examined by doctors in Atlanta where they lived, they considered that he might have encephalitis or another type of inflammation of the brain. After extensive investigations by several doctors, they turned to Emory University Hospital, where the doctors concluded that Christopher had a malignant tumor of the brain stem.

I say "concluded" because, although their doctors conducted CAT scans, they could not even see the brain stem. They could see only a horrible, malignant-appearing lesion.

"It's an inoperable condition," one of the doctors told Neil and Carol Pylant.

"What do you mean by that?" Neil asked, although he probably already knew.

"My advice is to take your son home. Make him as comfortable as possible and wait."

"Wait? Wait for him to die?"

"I'm afraid so."

"No!" Neil Pylant said, "God can heal our son."

"You don't understand," the doctor said. "He's, well, he's—he can't live much longer—"

"I don't care about the diagnosis," Neil said firmly. "God gave us this child. I'm ready to believe that God will heal him."

From Emory, the Pylants took young Christopher to several medical centers, all of which offered the same diagnosis. "Just do the best for him," they advised. "Let the boy die at home in comfort."

Carol and Neil would not settle for that word of doom. They contacted faith healers across the United States. Anyone they heard of who could heal the sick, they wrote to, phoned, or visited. Meanwhile, Christopher continued to deteriorate.

I first met the Pylants in late 1984 when they came to Johns Hopkins. "I felt impressed to bring him here," Neil said in his soft Southern accent. "We prayed for God to lead us to a Christian neurosurgeon who could help our boy." (He had not heard of me before.)

Christopher lay on a stretcher, scarcely breathing and barely moving. He was a pale, blonde child, almost a skeleton, with his eyes crossed. He looked so pitiful.

"Here are the X-rays," Neil said as he handed me a large envelope. "We brought them ourselves."

I took the X-rays, held them up to the light, and said, "This looks like a diffuse brain stem tumor." I paused long enough to look at the parents. "A diffuse tumor of the brain stem isn't anything that an operation will cure. I'm sorry, but there's nothing I can do about this."

"Doctor Carson," Neil said, "we know that the Lord is going to heal our son. We came here to Johns Hopkins after much prayer. We felt that if we came here with our son, we would find a Christian neurosurgeon who could help Christopher. When we learned that you are a Christian, we knew we had come to the right place."

"We believe this is going to happen," said Carol who, as I would learn, spoke little. Yet, the quietness of her voice only emphasized the strength of her conviction.

Frankly, the parents' attitude took me aback. I had never before or since encountered parents who talked with such an obviously sincere conviction. Although I honestly couldn't give them a single bit of hope, I wanted to do something. Finally I said, "Here's what I'll do. I'll at least show the X-rays to the radiologists. Maybe they can see something that I don't."

"Anything, Dr. Carson," Neil said. "I know God is going to use you."

The radiologists studied the X-rays and said, "Looks like a diffused brain stem tumor."

"I wonder," I said, "if we could do more scans. Perhaps an MRI*? See if there's any possibility of something other than a diffused brain stem tumor?"

He shrugged. "Okay. Why not?"

We put Christopher through MRI scans. Afterward, it still did not look like anything other than a diffused brain stem tumor, and that is exactly what I told the parents.

---

* Magnetic Resonance Imaging

"But, Doctor Carson," Neil said, "the Lord is going to heal him, and He's going to use you to do it."

"I don't know how God is going to do that," I said, trying to be honest without adding to their pain, "because I can't come up with any good rationale for doing anything more. Please try to accept that every test we've done only confirms that this tumor is inoperable."

"Please, Doctor, you can do something more," Neil insisted. "I know that God is going to use you to heal our son."

I can't recall the rest of the conversation, but I was feeling increasingly pressured, and more unsure of what else to do. "I'm impressed with your faith, but I can't do anything."

"The Lord is going to heal our son. We have no question about it. We know it's going to happen." With no false bravado, no yelling, Neil Pylant spoke quietly and with utter conviction.

"Okay," I said, "let me think." Partially I may have been yielding to Neil Pylant's pressure, but it was something more that made me determined to come up with a remedy. That something more was the unquestioning faith I saw in that mother and father. "I'll tell you what. You've come all this way. I can biopsy the lesion. By doing that, we can discover the exact tumor type. From there maybe we can administer some radiation or chemotherapy to prolong your son's life."

"Just do whatever you think—"

"Please understand this. If Christopher goes into the operating room, he will still be alive, but he may not have what I call a quality existence. But you seem to be out for any kind of existence. Is that what you're saying?—what you're willing to settle for?—any kind of existence whatsoever?"

"Yes, we want you to try anything," Neil said. "Because we know that when you get him in that operating room, God will heal him through you."

"Under those circumstances—your understanding the worst possible results—I will biopsy it."

I was not feeling optimistic. I wanted to do something to persuade them to go back home and be satisfied. A day or so later I took Christopher into surgery. As I lifted the cerebellum to get down to the area of the brain stem, I saw nothing but a horrible, gray, malignant-appearing lesion. I took a specimen—what we call a frozen section—and sent it to the lab. Within minutes the pathologist gave us a preliminary report of a high-grade astrocytoma (a highly malignant brain tumor).

"As long as we're here," I said to the surgery team, "let's remove as much of it as we can."

I started removing the tumor. After a while I began to see numerous vital structures, cranial nerves, and big blood vessels. "Time to stop," I said.

The danger was that if I proceeded, I might damage normal fibers of the brain stem, which would further harm Christopher, who was already in such a sad shape that I did not want to add to his problems.

After closing things up, I went immediately to the Pylants. I felt both sad and uncomfortable. I repeated what some would call the usual platitudes. Mainly I just did not know what else to say. They had been so sure that I could remove the tumor.

After explaining what I had found, I said, "Look, I don't know why your son has this horrible malignancy. It can't be removed. Perhaps your son has already served his purpose in life. Only God knows the beginning and the end. Maybe you shouldn't question the reason for these things."

"Thank you, Dr. Carson. I know you're sincere," Neil said, "but the Lord is going to heal our son. I just know it."

"Your faith is admirable," I said, hardly believing that they could still declare so staunchly that God was going to heal their son. Not one flicker of doubt clouded their faces.

These people are religious fanatics, I thought as I left them. *They just won't understand, but I guess they'll find out soon enough.* As a matter of course, I fully expected that Christopher would continue to deteriorate and probably die in the hospital.

Instead, Christopher got better—and no one was more surprised than I. His level of alertness improved, both eyes started to focus in the same direction, the difficulty with secretions disappeared. He moved more on his bed.

"What's going on here?" I asked myself. A day later I could not believe the tremendous difference in the boy. I turned to the nurse and said, "Let's get another scan." We did another CAT scan and a MRI. I could still see a large amount of the horrible tumor in the area of the brain stem. As I inspected more closely, however, I saw a small ribbon of tissue in one of the corners. Is it possible, I wondered, that the brain stem was up there? Can it be that the tumor is *outside* the brain stem? That it's crushing and pushing the brain stem up there?

Before the surgery, there had been so much tumor that I could not even see the brain stem. *Is it possible that the tumor has started to recede so that I can see some of the brain stem?* I knew the only way to find out.

"We'd better go back in," I told the parents.

"Praise the Lord," Neil said so quietly that I had to strain to hear the words.

Carol's eyes filled with tears. "Oh, thank you, thank you," she said.

Back to the operating room, buoyed by the confidence that there was a ribbon of brain stem, I started sucking away tumor tissue. I found pockets and pockets of the mass. It had insinuated itself into every possible crevice and crack. Eventually I saw the ribbon of brain stem.

"There it is!" I said aloud. To my delight, I discovered that it really was the brain stem I had seen, and it was intact. It had become almost flattened, but once I removed the tumor it filled in the area. As I continued to work, I could hardly believe what I had discovered.

Over the next five weeks the boy continued to get better.

In the meantime, the neuro-oncologist and the radiation therapist, of course, also received the pathology reports of this astrocytoma. Quite understandably, they felt that it was a highly malignant tumor. "Clearly, we need to give this patient radiation or chemotherapy or both," they said to me.

I explained to Neil and Carol, adding, "That is normal medical procedure—"

"No," Neil said.

"I'm against it," Carol said.

"The Lord has healed our son! Christopher is healed and he doesn't need any of that."

"At this stage, I'm willing to listen to you," I said. "As you well know, I would never have gone this far if you had not insisted—"

"Demanded," Neil said with a smile.

A few days later, Christopher left the hospital. He walked out to the car with nearly as much grace as any other child four years old.*

Months later, one of the doctors who was working as a neuro-oncologist told me, "You may not understand what's happened to me, Ben. You see, I've been an atheist for a long time. Or maybe I just did not see any need for God. But the Christopher Pylant incident has changed my thinking. The faith of those people and the results in that boy have had a profound effect on me." His words touched me just as much as his being honest enough to admit it. "I do understand the profound effect," I said.

"There's got to be something to religion," he said. "In fact, more than this. Honestly, this has made me a believer."

Aside from the special story of Christopher Pylant and my colleague's opening himself to God, I had also been deeply touched.

---

* Today, six years later, Christopher is neurologically normal.

Until that point I had considered myself a Christian physician. I prayed and went to church regularly. God was in my life without question. All the same, I had been extremely well trained, was quite smart, and knew that I was especially capable. That totaled up to mean that I actually believed that if anybody could do something, I was the one who could do it. Had not my mother said to me many times, "Bennie, you can do anything they can do—only *you* can do it better!"?

Through that childhood message from my mother, and from my training, I felt confident—maybe just a little cocky. After that episode with the Pylant family, however, I saw things differently. I still knew I was well-trained and capable, yet I also admitted that God had played a very big role in my life. From then on, I had an overwhelming sense that *if* I would allow Him to, God would play a big role in my career.

Although such an experience may be understandable to many, this was a revelation for me. It was as if I had prayed for God's help but either did not expect it, did not appreciate it when it was at work, or unconsciously denied the divine intervention.

Most of the significant cases I wrote about in *Gifted Hands* took place after the Pylant case. For example, in 1985 I met brown-haired Miranda Francisco, who was having up to one hundred seizures every day. She was four years old.

Dr. John Freeman, Director of Pediatric Neurology at Hopkins, and I discussed a hemispherectomy—a surgical procedure to remove half of the brain. Although it had been pioneered decades earlier, it had been all but abandoned. Insomuch as we knew that she would certainly die if we did not do the surgery, we decided to go ahead with it. Miranda underwent the surgery and recovered. Through a process called *plasticity,* the remaining half of the brain has taken over the functions of the missing portion.

In 1986, I did the intrauterine surgery on the Kyle twins. Of course, the best-known surgery was the separating of the Binder boys—the Siamese twins joined at the back of the head.

It has become abundantly clear to me that the Lord was letting me know through that experience with Christopher Pylant that He is there for me, available to be used if I call on Him.

I have called on God much more frequently since that experience.

Five

Taking Risks

> *Let not young souls be smothered out*
> *Before they do quaint deeds*
> *And fully flaunt their pride . . .*
> —*Vachel Lindsay*

S*ometimes giving our* best and Thinking Big involves risk. This is certainly true in my field. I think of it as doing what I know is right even when I have no assurance of the results. I do what some regard as adventuresome things because my actions at least give a dying person a chance to live.

In this chapter I want to describe three individuals who were high-risk cases, which made them controversial, but on whom we did the surgeries anyway.

First, there was an infant boy named Dusty Phillips.

Dusty came to us in 1985 from West Virginia with what we call a "primitive neuroectodermal tumor," that is, a highly malignant tumor on one hemisphere of the brain. Such tumors, usually fatal, are extremely fast-growing.

Neurosurgeons in West Virginia had biopsied the tumor and then given the child a few courses of chemotherapy, yet the tumor continued to progress.

In this kind of situation, when a biopsy or partial resection has been done and the tumor has been labeled as an aggressive malignant lesion, physicians treat it with chemotherapy. If the tumor does not decrease, doctors usually have to say, "We have done all we can. Just make the patient comfortable."

"Make the patient comfortable," means, of course, that they expect the person to die soon. They have exhausted everything they

89

know to reverse the situation, but nothing has produced any improvement. The one other piece of advice they gave in Dusty's case and without giving the family much hope, was, "Try Johns Hopkins. If there is anything that can be done, they are the ones who will know. They are doing some new kinds of surgery there."

It was the word of hope the parents needed. They brought the infant to our clinic. In evaluating Dusty Phillips, I agreed with the diagnosis of his physicians in West Virginia.

"However," I told them, "there is a slight chance for your son. Not a very big one, but—"

"Please, Dr. Carson," said the boy's father, Peter Phillips. "If you can do anything to help him, please try."

For a long time I spoke quietly with the parents, not wanting to raise false hopes. As I explained what I could do, I wanted to make certain they understood that we would be taking significant surgical risks. "I would attempt a large resection of the malignant tumor." Dusty was then almost a year old. The longer we waited, the greater the risk.

Before they made their decision, I told them, "The risk of significant or even fatal bleeding is substantial. We also have to face the possibility of infection, particularly in Dusty's case. He's already been weakened by chemotherapy and can't fight off a serious infection. You also need to think about the risk of a neurological impairment."

"What does that mean?" asked Mrs. Phillips.

"Paralysis. There's a strong possibility of partial or even complete paralysis. And something more. There's also the possibility of sensory changes. You see, Dusty could end up with significant visual disturbances or changes in his personality. He could even go into a coma."

"We want to do whatever we can," said the husband, confused, worried, and wanting the best for his child.

Mrs. Phillips looked directly at me and asked, "But what will happen if you don't do this? If you don't take the risk?"

Just as she spoke, I remembered so clearly the words of Dr. Taren that I had heard years before. I almost could hear his voice say, "Sure, it's a dangerous procedure, but look at the alternative if we do nothing." As I looked at her, I repeated those words. The husband nodded slowly. His wife said, "Then do it."

Dusty's extensive lesion involved a large part of the hemisphere. By then, I had done several hemispherectomies and felt that we should do a subtotal hemispherectomy (removal of less than one-half of the brain). Few other surgeons had attempted such a procedure, called a radical (or experimental) procedure. I knew all that, but I had had success. Although I had done such a surgery only a few times, I had met with no failures. My idea was to remove every part of the brain affected in any way by the tumor.

That is what we did, including cutting away the dura (the covering of the brain). Subsequently, the oncologist treated the child with another course of chemotherapy by using a combination of medications that our own group had come up with. The tumor never came back.

It has been five years now and Dusty is normal. He is neurologically intact also, with no evidence of any more tumors.

With Dusty we took risks, which I explained in advance to his parents. We gave our best and the risks paid off. The results encouraged us so much that the next time we saw a similar child, we were able to consent to the same operation with no hesitation because we had become sufficiently confident that we could use the same knowledge and experience we had gained from the radical resection of Dusty's brain.

❖ ❖ ❖ ❖

Second is the story of David Troutman. I include him as an example of Thinking Big and giving one's best because the medical professionals were not willing to give up on him. All of us involved were willing to take whatever risks necessary. The surgeon who had first worked with him, and the neuro-oncologist kept trying. All three of us knew that he faced the worst possible prognosis. Despite David's deteriorating condition, he was also determined to fight for his life. He had a primary tumor of the brain stem.

Another neurosurgeon at Hopkins had biopsied and diagnosed the tumor and then given David radiation. Because the tumor continued to grow, after two years the neurosurgeon involved switched David over to chemotherapy. He hoped it would at least bring the tumor under control. In 1988, David reached the stage at which we had to keep increasing his steroids. The lesion (tumor) still appeared to be progressing.

I hardly know how to describe the appearance of David Troutman when I first met him in 1988. At age twenty-one, he was older than most of my patients. Previously, he had been active, rather handsome, and had worked as a mechanic. All of that had changed since his diagnosis in 1984. Because of the steroids, his whole body was bloated, and he had to stay in a wheelchair.

His doctor and I, along with other members of the neuro-oncology team, concluded that the lesion we had studied many times on MRI* appeared to have borders to it. It was clearly into the brain stem.

"Why not go after it?" I asked after we completed all our examinations and tests.

"You've already had success with some brain-stem operations," my colleague said. "The patients survived. So I agree."

"At least there's a chance of taking it out without completely

---

* One way to explain a brain stem tumor is to think of mixing red sand with blue. When the two mix, the color diffuses or spreads throughout the brain stem in this case. Our scans indicated that the red and blue sands had not diffused. We could see distinct "margins" or areas. When we can see the distinctiveness, to my thinking, it is sometimes worth trying surgery.

destroying the patient," someone else said. So we decided to go in. As I had expected, we faced a difficult surgery.

Getting to David's brain stem was no simple matter. Years of scarring from previous surgery and from chemotherapy and radiation therapy had changed the consistency of the tissue to something hard and bloody. We felt distinct borders and margins on the tissues as they changed from one plane to the next. I explain this by saying that it would be like digging through an enormous bucket of sand, looking for a marble filled with nitro-glycerin. You could not just go madly plowing through it, because you might strike it with force that would cause an explosion and irreparable damage.

Finally I did extract tissue from the brain stem.

David had a stormy post-operative course—stormy in the sense that he had problems with his lungs, bouts of pneumonia several times, problems with bowel function, recurring fevers, and even complications with the shunt we had put in. But David never gave up. His courage inspired me and all of the people involved with his case.

I recall one low point at which a doctor from another service came to see David. Probably trying to be helpful and not allow him to raise false hopes, the doctor said, "You'll never be able to swallow again. You'd better face the fact that you'll always have to be fed through a tube in your stomach."

"Well, you're wrong," David said as forcefully as he could with his already weak voice. "I'm going to swallow again. And I'll do everything else I want to do."

Where David got his spunk, I don't know, but he never quit believing in his own recovery. His confidence pushed the rest of us forward. We knew we couldn't give up as long as David was still fighting.

David remained in the hospital four months. I'm happy to report that not only is he swallowing, but David is now walking.

He has lost the bloat and weight that resulted from having taken all the steroids. He speaks with a strong voice. Generally, he is doing quite well.

"I'm never going to give up," he said several times—and I knew that he meant it.

The story of David Troutman brings out part of my philosophy about giving one's best and Thinking Big. As long as an individual has a chance for reasonable quality of life but is deteriorating despite treatment, it is worth doing whatever possible to help. In these instances, I believe in intervening with radical treatment even if it is dangerous. After all, I remind myself, the alternative is continued deterioration and ultimately death.

Of course, it might have been easier to admit defeat in the David Troutman case, but I could not give up. Neither could his own physician and the other neurosurgeon.

"We've got to try," one of us said. That simple sentence expressed the feelings of all of us.

When he came to Hopkins, David was dying. It was our chance to help. When there is a chance, no matter how small, that is when, I believe, we must take risks and do everything that we can to maintain that high quality of life.

❖　❖　❖　❖

The third story is about a girl named Amber Kyle.

My involvement began with a phone call. "Ben," said Phil Goldstein, a Baltimore obstetrician, "I'd really like your advice on this one. We're taking care of a patient who is expecting twin girls."

Then he told me the problem. "By ultrasound, we've diagnosed that one of them has a rapidly expanding head from hydrocephalus."

It was the summer of 1986. Phil Goldstein said that the head was expanding so rapidly that he and his colleagues feared that it would force the mother into premature labor before the infants were capable of existing outside of the womb.

"What do you suggest?" he asked. "Do we intervene?"

"Yes," I said, "it's really the one chance we have."

The only way we would be able to prevent premature labor was to perform a procedure to alleviate the hydrocephalus while the babies were still *in utero* (in the uterus). The problem was that surgeons had not done such surgical procedures. Even so, I believed that it could be done, and Phil Goldstein was inclined to agree with me.

To get more background and information, we talked to another neurosurgeon, Robert Broadner, who was then practicing in Florida. Phil and I knew of research he had done in this area when he was living in Philadelphia. Broadner had invented a special type of shunt that he implanted in lambs and other animals while they were still inside the womb. Although this procedure had worked successfully, he had never tried it in a human.

Phil Goldstein and I flew to Florida and met with Bob Broadner. Together we worked out a technique that all three of us felt comfortable in trying.

At first I thought of doing it at Hopkins. However, since it was still considered experimental surgery, we would have to go through a lengthy procedure to get approval—and quantity of time we did not have in this case. Fortunately, Phil Goldstein had already been working with the ethics committee and other committees at Sinai, and another Baltimore hospital, who all knew about the problem.

"Can we do it at Sinai?" I asked.

"Why not?" Phil answered. "We're already set up for it."

For me to do this at Sinai meant that I had to get special permission for a one-time procedure, and then I had to have Johns Hopkins insure me. I talked to Don Long, which I would have done anyway. He reacted exactly as I had expected.

"What's your rationale?" he asked, which was really a rhetorical question, but I was prepared.

"If we do not do anything," I answered simply, "there's an excellent chance that both babies will be lost. If we do something, the worst result is that only the baby whose head we have to puncture *in utero* will be lost. Potentially, it means that the other, at least, would be saved."

I put it that simply. If Phil and I did nothing, both babies would probably die. By using the shunt, at least one of them would have a chance. In the back of my mind, of course, I hoped that we could save both.

"I'm behind you all the way," Don said, reacting exactly as I had expected. "I think it would be a compassionate and beneficial act to intervene." Don said this even though he knew, as I did, that it was controversial. (The controversial aspect is that some people quite sincerely believe that it is unethical to do experimental surgery on human patients. And this was experimental.)

All of us involved in the attempt to save both babies agreed to keep quiet about what we were going to do. We didn't want the media pressure that would surely erupt as soon as they heard about it. Secretively, we went ahead with the shunt that Dr. Broadner had invented.

Phil Goldstein inserted a large hollow tube, the same type used to do amniocentesis (the procedure obstetricians use to test the fluid surrounding a baby in the mother's womb). He then passed another tube with a series of even smaller tubes into the hydrocephalic baby's ventricle. Using ultrasound, we were able to see our actions on the television screen.

Then all of us paused momentarily. Those few seconds seemed to go on forever before Phil let out a big sigh. Then we nodded to each other. On the monitor-screen, we could actually see the head shrinking.

"It works," I said to Phil. "It works!"

I could only see his eyes because of the surgical mask, but the triumph in them was a joyous moment to cherish.

Although excited, we still didn't want to say anything to anybody. We didn't want this newsworthy event to get out until after we were certain there would be no setbacks.

The mother had experienced no difficulties during the procedure or afterward. After waiting three weeks, we decided that the lungs of both girls had matured appropriately. We took the babies through C-section. At that point, we discovered that not only was the normal baby moving fine but that the hydrocephalic baby was also moving and functioning quite well neurologically. Immediately, I placed a standard shunt in the twin named Amber.

On the day of the twins' birth, Phil and I allowed the procedure to become public information. The Sinai Hospital set up a news conference. The room filled with representatives from a wide range of newspapers and TV stations. As a matter of fact, my wife, Candy, had a delightful surprise when she saw part of the interview that night on the CBS evening news.

Unfortunately, the successful result did not end with everyone's being happy. The day after the news broke, criticism started to trickle in. Although both babies survived, most people did not know the details. Critics accused us of doing unsafe, experimental surgery. Despite trying to make it clear that at least one of the babies would have died, not everyone listened.

To make it worse, only a short time before this, the *New England Journal of Medicine* had just printed an article advising against such a procedure, calling it "highly experimental." The article said that most of the experimental results had been disastrous and that we were not ready for such experimentation at this stage of the medical game.

From those at Johns Hopkins I did not receive criticism. By then, I had already performed at least six hemispherectomies. We'd had so much press coverage over the hemispherectomies that people were acceptant that we did adventurous procedures when we felt that it saved lives.

Months later, when it became clear that *both* babies were doing extremely well, the critics were mature enough to reverse themselves. "Under those circumstances," they said, "it was the right thing to do." One of the critics even said, "Certainly, under those circumstances I think I would have done the same thing."

Of course I am pleased that the critics vindicated us. But, frankly, their censure did not matter very much. *We* knew we had done the right thing.

That's the important part of this story. We not only gave our best—Phil, Bob, and I, as well as all those who worked with us—but we did what we believed was right. Doing the right thing when it is not popular or when it is not going to get everyone's approval is not always easy, but I am convinced that if we truly care about other people, we will go ahead and take the risk anyway.

An epilogue: Both girls have continued to do extremely well. We did have to do subsequent surgery on Amber (two shunt revisions). She had a very large head, so we actually did a reduction (cranioplasty) to reduce the size of her head and to contour the shape. Amber is now a beautiful little four-year-old girl—and a healthy one—although she does have occasional seizures.

Six

Not Enough

If I shoot at the sun, I may hit a star.
—P. T. Barnum

Despite the difficulty involved and the lengthy ten hours in the operating room, the surgery had gone well. That night I went home drained. About two o'clock, the phone rang.

"Pressman *sneezed,*" said one of the residents.

"Oh, no," I groaned as I hung up and got dressed.

Working with Robert Pressman,* an oncology nurse at Johns Hopkins, turned out to be an invaluable experience for me—but in a way quite different from what I would have imagined.

Robert learned that he had a malignant tumor of the paranasal sinuses that extended up to the base of the brain. A talented surgeon and an ENT (Ear, Nose, and Throat) specialist at Hopkins, John Price, worked with me to perform a cranial facial resection. This operation usually takes eight to twelve hours because we have to go in through the front of the head and the nose.

We had to open the face and the head to get one of the tumors, situated deep in the head along the base. It might help to understand what we did if I use the image of a chandelier. (In fact, I call it the chandelier operation.)

It works this way. If I went into an old house to remove a big chandelier, first I'd be sure I had people on the first floor ready to receive it. Above the fixture I would make cuts to disconnect. I'd then have someone on the second floor with me to cut a hole around the chandelier fixture. Once done, I could drop the whole thing to the people below.

---

* To protect the privacy of the people involved, I have used different names.

Using that analogy, one doctor detaches the tumor from everything on the first floor while the neurosurgeon, working above, lifts up the brain and disconnects the tumor from everything along the skull base before dropping it below. Then the tumor can be pulled out through the face.

After Rob Pressman sneezed, he started going downhill physically. "Mentally, he seems disoriented," the resident said.

Before I got back to the hospital, they took X-rays. The results showed a tremendous amount of air in his skull. We concluded that when he sneezed, Rob had blown the air upward and into his cranium. This caused a contusion (bruising) of the brain. He continued to decline.

We started doing everything we could to reduce the cranial pressure and to reduce the amount of air. Air had been forced into the cranial cavity, which normally does not have any air in it. This was not only taking up space but had probably been forced in under significant pressure and, therefore, was pushing on the brain and had bruised the brain during its entrance.

Throughout the following week Robert continued to decline until he no longer responded to commands. We had to place a breathing tube in him.

Eventually his pupils became nonreactive and he lost his doll's eyes. (When we turn somebody's head and the eyes follow the motion of the head, which is normal, we call this "doll's eyes." When the eyes remain fixed with the head, it's a bad sign.)

It was looking pretty grim for Rob. As he continued his descent, most of us had about decided that it was the end of the line for him. I discussed his prognosis with his wife, Dolores, who is also a nurse at Hopkins.

Because of her training and her experience in ICU and in a neurosurgery unit, Dolores did not have much to learn from me that she did not already know.

She listened quietly to everything I said. For a few seconds she was silent. Then she said, "I understand."

"I'm sorry—"

"I concluded several days ago that he isn't going to recover," Dolores said. "This is a terminal situation." Ever the professional nurse, she refused to give way to her feelings. We continued to talk. It was obvious that she had worked through her immediate, personal pain. Her biggest concern was how to explain this tragedy to their three children. They were about the same ages as my three kids.

As we talked, I wondered how Candy would handle the situation.

"What do you think?" Dolores asked, interrupting my own thoughts. "Should the children be allowed to come into the hospital and see their daddy in this state? Or should they just remember him the way he was? How should they be told that he won't be coming home?"

Questions spilled out, and we spent a long time discussing the situation. Of course, the decision was hers to make, and she hadn't really been asking me to decide. I think it was simply that she needed to ask the questions aloud. Finally, Dolores decided not to bring the children to see Rob in the ICU.

All in all, Dolores handled this situation remarkably well. She asked all the practical questions and tried to make the wisest decisions. The strain showed, but she is a strong person.

By contrast, I was feeling horrible, although I don't think anyone picked up on that.

First, although I didn't know Rob well before he developed the disease, I had liked him. His dying would be a loss to me as a person. Even more, I realized that during the treatment and surgery, I had begun to identify too strongly with this guy—each of us being both the same age and the father of three children. His oldest child was eight years old, just a couple of years older than my oldest son.

Second, facing Rob's death had the curious and depressing

effect of making me think about myself and my family. It also triggered memories of my childhood, especially as I thought about a certain eight-year-old child.

The emotional memory of my own childhood pain flooded over me. I was eight years old when my parents divorced. That's when I admitted to myself that my father wouldn't be coming home at night anymore. I wouldn't have the joy of running down the street and meeting him when he came home from work. I'd never sit beside him in his car as he drove through the streets of Detroit. The loneliness I felt as a child without a father was just too real for me.

Then I wondered, *How would my boys feel if someone had to tell them that their dad would not be coming home anymore? That he wouldn't be able to play with them again? Or read to them? Take them for walks? How would my sons have reacted if someone had said, "Your daddy won't be coming back again"?*

I got caught up in identifying with Rob and could not shake the powerful feelings. Although the staff didn't know what was going on inside me, apparently they were sensitive enough to realize how concerned I was over this matter. They threw as much support toward me as they did to Dolores.

That afternoon I managed to switch things around so that I could leave before dark. I needed to get away from the clinic to think and to work through my own feelings. As I walked to the parking lot, I could not extinguish the emotion springing from the thought of what the loss of Rob would be to those three young children.

Getting into my car, I started driving home, hardly aware of the road or other vehicles. "Lord, have You got one more miracle You can pull out of this?" The words tumbled from my lips. "Those poor children. And Dolores. God—Oh, God, please do something."

As I drove out of Baltimore, my eyes swept across the countryside. I remembered that only months earlier, Rob and Dolores had been so excited about their plans. They had bought a nice tract of land, and at the time of Rob's diagnosis they had everything ready to start building their house. Now everything was falling apart.

As I continued to drive, I couldn't imagine those kids going through life without their father. And what about Dolores's loss? Would she have to struggle as my own mother had, by working more than one job at a time? Would her children see her wearied face and tired body when she came home late at night?

"Please, please, God, don't let this tragedy happen."

It was such a bizarre thing. To make it even worse to cope with, we had been able to get all of the malignancy. From a surgical standpoint, the operation had been a success. If only he hadn't sneezed . . .

"No," I said aloud, "he did sneeze. He is . . . terminal." And I hated the sound of that word.

The next day I was scheduled to leave for Atlanta to give the commencement address at Morehouse Medical School. Although I tried to concentrate on last-minute preparations for my speech, Rob, Dolores, and their children continued to weigh heavily on my mind.

Lord, I need a booster here, I remember praying. *You could do wonders for my faith right now. Somehow bring Rob out of this situation.* I do not know if I believed that God would do it or not; I did know that I had to ask.

Just before I left the hospital for the airport, a nurse called me. "Ben, could you talk to the grandparents? They've asked to see you."

"I can't," I said. "I've got to catch my plane. If I wait even five more minutes, I'll never make it."

That was true, but also I didn't think I could face them and talk about Rob right then. I was already so emotionally tied up, they'd probably have had to offer me comfort.

The grandparents needed to hear from an authority figure and to receive comfort, but I simply didn't have time. In fact, the telephone call had disrupted me and I left a few minutes later than I had planned. I had to rush to make my plane. As I sped toward the airport, I also had to cope with the added pain of guilt.

Somehow I made it through the weekend, speech and all. When I returned to Baltimore, Rob was still heavily on my mind. Before going home, I rushed over to the intensive care unit. I entered his cubicle and noted that he didn't seem to have changed in any way. He was still on the respirator. I observed no movements, and his eyes were closed.

With a sinking heart I began to examine him. I touched Rob's chest. Just then his hand shot up and touched mine. I stared at his hand. "That's a purposeful movement," I said to the nurse standing behind me. My voice was calm, but my heart was beating rapidly. I could hardly believe this.

I grabbed my flashlight, lifted his eyelids, and shone the light into them. His pupils reacted.

"What is this?" I asked. "Did you see that?" I touched Rob lightly and his hand moved toward me again. Just then I turned around and saw myself flanked by half of the ICU staff. "Rob moved. He moved his hand by himself."

The nurse, no longer able to suppress her delight, smiled. "We know. He started waking up last night."

"Are you serious? Nobody told me—"

"We knew how involved you were," she said. "All of us wanted to see your reaction when you came in."

That was the beginning of a rapid recovery. Within two days, Rob was off the respirator. He was soon talking and walking. His children came to see him, and I experienced a deep, peaceful joy as I watched him playing with them. For a father, nothing feels better than interacting with his little ones.

Rob completely recovered.

A few days later, one of the nurses came up to me. "Dr. Carson, there's another patient here who will probably expire. Would you lay hands on him, please?" It seemed obvious that she was only half-serious.

I shook my head. "Look, it's not me doing these things. God does all these things and can keep on doing them without me. If God is going to work a miracle, He certainly doesn't need me to do it."

I really believed it then. I still do.

A few days after Rob went home there was an interesting development. Since I first entered the field of medicine, I have met doctors who have difficulty dealing with unanswerable situations. Often they'll finally admit, "Well, there's some explanation, we just don't understand it."

One of the neurologists, an especially brilliant man and one who doesn't acknowledge a belief in God, pondered this matter of Rob for several days. He asked question after question, determined to figure out an answer. None of us could offer an explanation for Rob's recovery.

"Absolutely none," I said.

"I know, but I think I've finally figured it out," he said.

"Really?"

"Sure. Simple. It's the mitrochondria at the subcellular level, and they can go into shock." (That is, some of the energy producing parts of the cells that constitute the central nervous system had simply started functioning again at a normal level. Basically, it was like turning the lights down low, but not turning them completely off.)

I listened to his explanation before I asked him a question. "Tell me, did you ever see such a thing before?"

"No, not really, but—"

"This is a miracle," I said. "Why not accept it for what it is? They don't come any more blatantly than this. Rob was gone and now he's back. This is the only time I've ever seen an adult sink to such a low neurological level and then recover."

As my final statement I said, "We don't have to explain miracles; all we have to do is accept them."

The story of Rob Pressman, besides having a tremendous effect on me, has helped me discern still another facet of doing our best. All of us at the clinic had done our best. No matter how many times I reviewed the situation, there was nothing I could fault. We had done our best.

When we have done our best, we also have to learn that we still need to rely on God. Our best—no matter how good—is incomplete if we leave God out of the picture.

Even today, I do not have an explanation for Rob's recovery. I do have an answer, though: I prayed. Others prayed. When we knew that our best still would not cure Rob, God was the only alternative source of help.

Thanks, God, for honoring our best by giving us a miracle.

Part Two

You Can Give Your Best and Think Big

> *To be of use in the world is the only way to happiness.*
> —*Hans Christian Andersen*

Seven

Thinking Big

*Education is the best provision
for old age.*

—Aristotle

Think positively.

"Use PMA" (Positive Mental Attitude) — "Have faith" — "You are what you think." "I did it. So can you." Haven't we all been bombarded with these slogans for years? Even though we've heard them often, it doesn't make them less true. Or more real.

More and more of us in the medical field are realizing that our attitude is a stronger indicator of our pending recovery than our physical status or prognosis. A positive outlook determines so many variables.

No patient I ever had brought this truth home more clearly than Tony.

A young man barely out of his teens, Tony was a New Yorker of Italian descent. In 1985 he underwent an initial operation for a malignant brain tumor. A year later the tumor recurred. Tony's family brought him to Hopkins. I did radical surgery to remove most of the new growing tumor. Initially he did quite well, but he faced a recurring infection. Consequently, I had to remove not only the rest of the tumor but some of the bone flap as well.

To our surprise, Tony did amazingly well. Soon he was home and fully functional. He even started driving a car again. Here at Hopkins, we followed Tony's case. Frankly, we couldn't quite figure out why he was doing so well—he had far outlived the statistical odds. We did notice that he had a strong, positive attitude and often said, "I'm going to beat this thing, you know."

While he was going through all of this, Tony had a girlfriend who stuck by him. They planned to marry eventually. Although I don't know the reason, a year or so after Tony had recovered from surgery the girlfriend broke up with Tony.

That breakup left him so crushed that Tony lost his optimistic spirit and slid into a spirit of depression. Within weeks the tumor had grown back. Then Tony died.

My purpose in relating this incident is to point out what a tremendous role our attitude plays in our well-being as well as in our ability to fight disease. Few today would question that our emotional state affects hormones in our body. Hormones significantly influence white cells and the body's ability to fight disease. This means that we now actually have a scientific explanation for the fact that people who become very depressed do not do well in recovering from disease.

As Proverbs puts it, "As he thinketh in his heart, so is he." (23:7 KJV). It also says, "A merry heart doeth good like a medicine: but a broken spirit drieth the bones" (17:22 KJV). If we think with a positive stance, we can actually influence our health, our mental attitude, and the way we relate to others.

I am certainly not suggesting that we run around with smiles on our faces all the time and repeat fifty-nine times a day, "I think positive thoughts," but as I perceive it, the right kind of thinking develops as we mature. If we allow ourselves to dwell on negatives, on hurts, on mistreatments, we will be negative thinkers.

We can choose the way we think. When people object to words like "positive thinking," I sometimes say, "Think Big, then!"

Thinking Big means opening our horizons, reaching for new possibilities in our lives, being open to whatever God has in store for us on the road ahead. Thinking Big is another way of restating one of my mother's favorite sayings: "You can do anything they can do—only you must try to do it better!" That's Thinking Big.

Over the years I have urged others to give their best, to seek for excellence, and to Think Big. One day I was mulling over those two words and I worked out an acrostic for it. Although the eight letters of *Think Big* do not express all my thoughts or put them in any particular order, the acrostic does provide a way for me to talk about the success in my life and about giving my best for others:

T = TALENT
H = HONESTY
I = INSIGHT
N = NICE
K = KNOWLEDGE
B = BOOKS
I = IN-DEPTH KNOWLEDGE
G = GOD

The **T** in **THINK BIG** stands for **TALENT.**

"Who, me?" I've heard people say when I speak about talent. "Oh, no, God passed me by on that one."

That is not true. All of us have talents, often undeveloped, sometimes ignored, and frequently used without our realizing that they are gifts to us from God.

It is not enough just to have abilities; we must learn to recognize them and use them appropriately. Because I sincerely believe this integral part of my thinking, I want to make a strong statement about the importance of Thinking Big.

T = TALENT

IF YOU RECOGNIZE YOUR TALENTS,
USE THEM APPROPRIATELY,
AND CHOOSE A FIELD THAT USES
THOSE TALENTS;
YOU WILL RISE TO THE TOP OF YOUR FIELD.

Does this mean that you will be an outstanding surgeon? Attorney? Entertainer? Not really. This principle recognizes that God endows each of us with some kind of ability. If we use that ability for good, we can become excellent in our field.

For example, Shirley is a copy editor who has an extraordinary ability to catch the little mistakes that many editors and readers overlook. My point is that being successful means striving for excellence no matter what the work. She enjoys checking grammar or adding and deleting punctuation marks. Because she's so skillful at what she does, Shirley has received several opportunities for advancement in her publishing firm. "No," she says. "Copyediting is what I do best. This is where I want to stay."

Or I think about Bill Cosby, an extremely intelligent fellow with a doctorate in education. Although I do not know him personally, I consider him an individual with tremendous insight into what is funny. I think that is a talent that he recognizes in himself—the ability to extract humor out of situations. Even though he has an academic background, it is as if he decided, "This is something I'm so good at that I'm going to make a career out of looking for humor." Obviously, he has become one of the premiere comedians in this country.

I admire the fact that in the midst of his fame, Cosby has not forgotten about other people. He emphasizes the need for education, has become involved in several educational programs, and donates his time and money to encourage young people. He is not urging them to become entertainers but to develop themselves intellectually.

My biggest gripe against people in sports and entertainment is that they do not, for the most part, try to emphasize intellectual development. I have heard many of them interviewed. The message that so often comes across goes like this, "I did it this way and you can do it, too." Or sometimes it has a boastful ring that implies, "If you were as good as I am, you'd be famous, too."

Unfortunately, that's just not true. When we consider someone's becoming an NBA basketball star, we're looking at odds of seven young people out of at least a million who make it to the NBA as starters. Even once they make it, we're still looking at an average career span of only two-and-a-half to three-and-a-half years—the *average* for all professional sports.

It saddens me to see the effort youngsters put into shooting baskets all day and night hoping to get to the NBA. What the NBA stars don't state is, "Yes, I have a lot of talent, but I also happened to be in the right place at the right time. Somehow I managed to make connections with the right people, and I have been incredibly lucky. Much of what has happened to make me famous didn't have much to do with my talent."

Many more people could play in the NBA if they had the same breaks. But who can guarantee equal-opportunity breaks in life? Yet we can do something meaningful and positive for ourselves by developing every part of ourselves, especially our intellectual abilities and our God-given talents. That is one way we also learn to make our own breaks.

Months ago I read the book *Green Power*, a self-published autobiography of a man from Birmingham, Alabama. Now in his nineties, Arthur (he prefers A. G.) Gaston had recognized his talent for business while he was quite young. In the 1920s, Gaston started a black-owned burial insurance company because he saw so many poor blacks treated unfairly. From a penniless beginning, he has become one of America's multimillionaires.

When I met A. G. Gaston, I asked him, "How did you become so rich, particularly as a black man in the Deep South at a time when being black took away every opportunity?"

"Not every opportunity," he answered. "That's part of my philosophy. First I saw a need. When I felt the deep-seated concern that people have about how they are going to bury themselves and their loved ones, I decided to do something about it."

Gaston promised people that if they signed up and agreed to pay him twenty-five cents a week, their burial would be taken care of when they died. The quarter a week was not much. Although some died before they paid in enough, expectedly, other people paid more. Gaston then took the profits and invested them.

Eventually Gaston realized that they needed a bank in Birmingham that extended loans to blacks, because none of those currently existing would give loans without exorbitant interest. Using the same philosophy of "I saw needs and then filled them," he got busy and, after getting financial commitments from other black leaders, he opened a bank.

This black man living in Dixie in a prejudiced society that made no allowances for minorities or didn't try to give them a boost, proved that talent works. In *Green Power,* Gaston admits that he has amassed vast sums of money, enabling him to do just about anything he has wanted to do and to go anywhere he has wanted to go.

Because Gaston recognized his ability to make money, he was able to tell me, "It wasn't a matter of white power or black power, but green power." By that he meant that he used his God-given talent to earn money. With his earned wealth, more doors opened, creating even more opportunities.

I cite the story of Gaston for several reasons:

1. *He never sought excuses.* Like most of the young men his age, he could so easily have felt sorry for himself, given up, or gone to work in a coal mine. Instead, he refused to surrender to all the excuses for failure.
2. *Gaston accepted his talent and used it.* Because he had the innate ability to amass wealth, he determined that no one or no barrier would stop him.
3. *He developed his talent together with helping other people.* Although I have listed it as third, this point is crucial.

Gaston did not look out only for himself in accumulating wealth. He began to move ahead when he saw needs around him.

Whenever Gaston observed unscrupulous business leaders taking advantage of poor and ignorant blacks in Alabama, it not only made him angry, but angry and committed enough to do something to change conditions. "I saw needs and I filled them."

If more of us were to adopt such an attitude—instead of relying on excuses for not doing something—who knows what we could accomplish.

Particularly when I speak to young people, I talk about talent. When I get the chance for a one-to-one or small-group conversation, I often ask, "What talent do you have?"

I have done this so often that I can now fairly well predict how they will respond. Their answers will come out like this:

> — "I can sing."
> — "I can play basketball."
> — "I'm good at sports."
> — "I play an instrument."

They tend to think in terms of being performers, superstar singers, or hotshot ball players. Seldom do I hear someone say, "I'm good at math," or "I'm a good reader." No one has yet answered me by saying, "I can extract complex concepts from the written page," or "I'm very good with computer science." Yet, these abilities *are* talents—gifts that not everyone possesses. Those same talents make each of us unique, and they can push us to see a need and do something to fill it.

When people offer excuses (and I hear umpteen of them when I talk about talent and motivation), it's because they don't stop to think that God has given to every one of us more than fourteen billion cells and connections in our brain. Now why would God give us such a complex organ system unless He expects us to use it?

I have attained quite a few goals in my own life but am the same person, with the same brain, that I was when no one else shared the academic bottom of my fifth-grade class with me. No one gave me a brain transplant so that I could be at the top of my seventh-grade class. No greater opportunities suddenly came my way.

What made the difference for me between fifth grade and seventh? My mother started my uphill climb. She said to me, as she had said countless times:

— "Ben, you are a smart boy. I want to see you using that smartness."
— "Ben, you become whatever you want to be in this life if you're willing to work at it."
— "I work among rich people, people who are educated. I watch how they act and I know you can do anything they can do. Bennie, you can do anything they can do—only you must try to do it better!"

Maybe everyone can't do it better—it is not a matter of competing with someone else. Essentially, it is accepting our own special abilities as special—and then developing them.

Most of us have ample capability in some area in our lives. When we understand that, we are beginning to discover our talents. Not everyone can do everything. Not everyone can be a neurosurgeon. Individuals who are not well-coordinated, for instance, even though very intelligent, won't make good neurosurgeons.

Some people need to have everything very concretely laid out, cannot see patterns, and cannot distinguish shades of differences. Such individuals might not make good radiologists, because a radiologist has to be able to see subtle changes.

I know individuals who do not have the ability to form a good argument. They know what they want to say but are not able to put it into appropriate words. If they stick with it and finally say what they really mean, it takes them a long time and demands much energy. Yet, they may be talented in another field— electronics, for example. They would not be suited for a career in law, but they might make fantastic computer-repair persons.

When I evaluate myself and my own talents, I realize that one special talent that I have been given is hand-eye coordination, combined with the ability to think in three dimensions. That gift, along with my interest in the brain, enabled me to say, "I should be a brain surgeon."

Perhaps I could have become a lawyer, or an engineer, but I don't think I would have excelled in those areas in the same way that I have excelled in neurosurgery. I wouldn't have taken advantage of my talents and my interests. In other words, to give an example, anyone with a normal brain has the capacity to do almost anything, but when one has special gifts or talents (and *everyone* has) and takes advantage of and develops these talents— that person is likely to excel. For instance, Johann Sebastian Bach could probably have become a doctor, but had he done so he would probably not have been taking maximum advantage of his talents as a musician, and therefore would not be widely known today. All of us need to discover our talents and choose careers that allow us to maximize those talents.

A simple method that I suggest to young people for discovering their intellectual talents is not just for young people—persons of any age can find it useful: Find a quiet place where it is possible to think and not be interrupted for a few minutes. Then do the following exercise.

The Exercise:

1. Ask yourself the questions below. It is helpful to write the answers. You can study them and think about them anytime.

2. In answering, be honest but also be generous. To do well at something does not mean you have to do it perfectly. It means that you do something well and that the results show that you do it well.

Even for those at the academic bottom of the class, the questions are still valid. *All of us can do something.*

 a. At what have I done well so far in life?

 b. In what school subjects have I done well?

 c. Why did I choose those subjects?

 d. What do I like to do that has caused others to compliment me?

 e. What do I do well and think of as fun although my friends see it as work—or as a boring activity?

3. Analyze yourself and your situation. As much as you can, analyze matters for yourself instead of depending upon tests and outside advice. However, I know that some people are not very good at self-reflection and do better by interacting with others. (By the way, part of the talent of people-centered individuals is to interact well with others!)

4. Whether you can figure out the answers to these questions, or you talk them over with someone else, find someone whose judgment is respected. Your parents, perhaps. A teacher. Your pastor. An older family friend. Your closest friend.

5. Write down what is said by those in whom you confide.

6. Compare those ideas to what you have written about yourself. Are the answers the same? What do you now see about yourself that you didn't think of before? For four or five days, spend some time each day by yourself in thinking about these answers.

Unfortunately, many people do not realize that almost nothing is ever accomplished by anyone without their having spent some time at it, thinking about it, and analyzing it. Most people won't stop to analyze. Some do not even know how to do it well. (Those who have trouble with self-analyzing probably need to get someone they trust to help them.)

I want to point out one big mistake I have noticed, particularly among the rising middle- and upper-middle-income families. The parents who themselves never achieved try to take over the lives of their children and decide their future for them. The same is true for families that push their children into areas of study in which they themselves have achieved, assuming that their children must follow the same occupation. In both instances, the parents are pushing, trying to channel the youngsters into areas for which they may have no talent.

For individuals to take a stand against that pressure is not easy. Immediately I think of my friend Hamilton Moses, III—we call him Chip Moses. His great-grandfather, grandfather, and father were all Harvard-trained lawyers. Quite naturally, the family fully expected Chip to be a Harvard-trained lawyer, too. Chip did go to Harvard, but he bucked the system. Instead of law, he chose medicine—and the family was not happy with his choice.

This man who stood against family expectations is a highly talented physician today. He also "happens" to be vice-president of Johns Hopkins Hospital. In the area of medicine, Chip has excelled because he recognized that his talents lie in the scientific sphere.

Chip is the kind of individual who declares, "I will not be channeled by history or family pressure into a certain area. I will stop and recognize my own talents and then use them appropriately."

This is what people must do, regardless of their socio-economic background. To make the most out of life, all of us need to stop, think (and analyze), and use the talents God has given us.

Once we start living an enriched life, we are better able to give our best and enable others to attain their best.

In the late spring of 1990, I received an invitation to speak to students of a middle school (grades 7–9) in Washington state. Although the school was not on a reservation, many of the native-American students who attended the school did live on one. Others came from families of migrant workers who were in the area for crop harvesting.

One of the teachers, although delighted to have me, also felt the need to warn me about what to expect: "Dr. Carson, we have a great number of drug problems in this school."

"So do many others, so—"

"But we also have a lot of crime and violence in the community."

"I understand," I said.

"Don't be disappointed or angry if your reception isn't what you had anticipated," said a school official. "Given their background, many of the students might not be particularly interested in what you have to say. They might be rude or—"

"Worse than that," another interrupted. "They might start throwing things at you."

"And I suppose you know about the recent murder," said a teacher.

"Yes," I answered. "Someone mailed me a newspaper clipping about it."

"Then you know they weren't just murdered, but the killers also had cut up their bodies."

"Yes," I said, "I know." They weren't helping me to get more excited about the meetings, but I did believe they were trying to prepare me for the worst. "I've taken all this under advisement."

At the assembly time, I followed the school officials into the gym. The entire student body erupted into the room, filling up bleachers as they pushed, shoved, and yelled at each other.

Strangely enough, as I watched, I felt nothing but a peaceful confidence, probably because I had prayed before accepting the invitation. And just as important, maybe it was because I felt I had something to share with those students.

After the principal introduced me, I stood up and walked toward the wooden podium. Without question, they were quite noisy. A few times I had to speak over their voices. Then I started to tell my story:

"By the time I was in the fifth grade, I had no competition for last spot in my class. I was not considered an intellectual giant by anyone, especially not by myself. I expected always to get the lowest grade. I expected always to be the first person to sit down when there was a spelling bee. I expected never to know the capital cities of any of the states or anything of that nature."

I paused, aware that a hush had fallen over the audience. I smiled at them as I remembered a story about a math class.

"One time I made a grade of D in a math class. You know what happened? My math teacher praised me. 'Oh, Bennie,' she said. 'That is such an improvement!'

"In case you don't know it, the D didn't stand for Delightful. But I was such a poor student, a D *did* seem like a delight next to all the Fs I kept getting. At midterm, when the report cards came out, I had to show my mother a long line of grades, with one D being my *highest* grade.

"My mother, not an educated woman herself, knew that she couldn't do anything, but she knew someone who could. She prayed; she talked to God and asked for wisdom."

Despite all the warnings by the faculty and administration, I have never had a more attentive audience. I knew that they understood, because I observed their faces, especially when I told them other stories about my embarrassment and self-hatred for being at the bottom of the class. "I didn't know there was anything better for me."

Their rapt attention was telling me that inside they were saying, "Hey, I can identify with that."

They continued to listen as I told them how my mother had forced me to read two books a week, how the school had provided eyeglasses so that I could see, and how I seemingly had jumped overnight from the bottom to the top of the class.

Next, I told them about my education and that today I am a surgeon. I could tell that they were flabbergasted as I started talking about performing hemispherectomies, about separating the Binder twins, and about a few of the brain-tumor operations. When I spoke of some of the desperate situations of the people who came into our clinics, many of them actually leaned forward.

Specifically I remember saying, "What a wonderful thing it is to be able to contribute to the restoration of someone's health. It's not only a feeling that I'm worth something, but that I have something to contribute."

After giving them an overview, I started talking about the complexity of the human brain, giving examples of the functions that the human brain can actually perform. Once again, amazement was written across their faces.

When I finished, I started to step away. Just then I saw a few of the big boys on the top row stand. They started to clap. Within seconds, that once-rough, noisy, rowdy crowd gave me a standing ovation.

When the principal finally dismissed them, the students mobbed me, asking questions, wanting autographs, and begging for permission to have their picture taken with me.

I was surprised; the officials were amazed.

As I have thought of that experience, I have a feeling that most of those officials assumed that, given the students' background and environment, they accepted their poverty and their bleak future. From their well-meant warnings, I felt that they held out little encouragement for the students because they didn't think that the students could hope for more than what they had right then.

I hope my impressions were wrong. I hope that the leaders of the school saw promise in those students and offered them hope.

The fact is, it does not matter what group of individuals I talk to—everyone wants and *needs* to hear words of hope. All of us need to have someone say to us, "You can do it. You can achieve."

As I think back to my fifth-grade experience, I did not behave as though I wanted to achieve. Most of my classmates probably assumed that I didn't care. How mistaken they were!

The fact that individuals sometimes act as if they do not want to achieve, or they are belligerent, stems from the reality that they are afraid of what might happen if they do try. They are afraid of failure; they have no vision of success. *What else can we expect?* they are silently asking. I believe their seeming indifference is a cover-up for their real feelings.

It certainly was true for me.

Frequently I remind myself as I remind others, that we have a responsibility to take these youngsters under our wings, to help them realize that they do have intellectual talents. *Coming from an ethnic minority or a lower socio-economic class has nothing to do with our innate ability.* There are brilliant (even if uneducated) people living on Indian reservations and in migrant camps, just as there are brilliant people living in Beverly Hills and Hyde Park.

Sometimes young men, in particular, try to adopt a "macho" image as a substitute for academic and intellectual achievement. It is easier for them to pattern themselves after such images as Rambo, Shaft, and Terminator, because they see them all the time and because it requires less intellectual effort for them to imitate examples like Kurt Schmoke (the Rhodes Scholar mayor of Baltimore), Enrico Fermi (the renowned physicist), or Colin Powell.

In the few years I have practiced at Johns Hopkins, I have come into contact with many resident doctors. Many are quite good; a few are extremely gifted like Art Wong whom I mentioned earlier.

Currently we have a highly gifted resident named Raphael Tamargo. An Hispanic, Raphael comes from an under-represented minority in the medical field. He is quite short, with a slim build, and he speaks with an obvious Hispanic accent. It would be easy for some to pass him by just for those reasons. Yet Raphael, aside from being an extremely nice person, is very, very bright.

He graduated from medical school at Columbia Presbyterian Hospital, Columbia University in New York. While still a medical student, he did outstanding research work, and we later accepted him into our program. For three years, Raphael worked in the laboratory, received grants from the American Association for Brain Tumor Research, and won awards for his research in treating malignant brain tumors.

Now out of the lab, Raphael has become a favorite person of the staff and the nurses because he is so thorough in everything he does. Some might call him compulsive because he insists that everything be done correctly. If anyone gives his best for others, it is Raphael.

I have no doubt that Raphael will stay in the field of academic neurosurgery. By making significant contributions to the field, he has already proved his talent. I am proud to be associated with this man from a racial minority that many people do not think of as making great intellectual contributions in a field like neurosurgery. He has proved them wrong.

To sum up: If we recognize our talents and use them appropriately, and choose a field that uses those talents, we will rise to the top of our field.

Eight

Honesty Shows

> *An honest man's the noblest work of God.*
>
> —*Robert Burns*

One of my classmates in pre-med at Yale graduated *magna cum laude*—no small attainment at any Ivy-League school. However, I saw one basic character flaw in the man: He wasn't honest. The fellow flagrantly disregarded rules and regulations that as a student he had promised to observe. Frequently he broke curfew regulations and often had women in his room overnight at a time when such was not permitted.

Many of our examinations were the closed-book type—examinations based on the honor code. The professor gave out the examination and often left the room. During those exams, I often saw this classmate opening his book, as did other students. Yet, he didn't seem to worry that anyone of importance would notice.

It was bad enough that he behaved in such a flagrantly disobedient manner, but even more lamentable was the fact that he didn't show any sign of feeling guilty, acting as though it were some kind of game.

The day of honest reckoning came, however. Of all the pre-med students I knew at Yale, he was the only one not accepted into any medical school!

It is a strange behavior pattern—how people deceive themselves, thinking that no one will unmask their dishonesty, that they can hide in the crowd. Yet, I am convinced that we do not really get away with anything. I am not sure that we all get repaid in this life for every dishonest deed we do, but I am convinced that we all harvest the fruits of our labors.

Here is another way of looking at it:

> Do not be deceived: God cannot be
> mocked. A man reaps what he sows. The
> one who sows to please his sinful nature,
> from that nature will reap destruction;
> the one who sows to please the Spirit,
> from the Spirit will reap eternal life. Let
> us not become weary in doing good, for
> at the proper time we will reap a harvest
> if we do not give up (Galatians 6:7–9).

We may think we won't be unmasked or that we can hide in the crowd, but we are only deceiving ourselves. Whereas we all make mistakes and we all fail at one time or another, my classmate thought he could cover up everything and incur no ill effects on his life.

He was wrong.

Most of us knew the kind of person he was. To his obvious surprise, the professors did, too, which just goes to show that when a pattern of dishonesty develops in our lives, it can only be detrimental in the long run.

Conversely, some people may be too honest. I think of my uncle, William Avery, as the most ethical and guileless man I know. Scrupulously honest and truthful, Uncle William felt that he always had to tell the truth (sometimes his perception of the truth may have been a little distorted because he certainly did not have any formal education). Although he is not a sophisticated individual, I deeply admire his keen sense of honesty.

At one point in his life, when he first went into business, he began with a simple buying and reselling plan. His honesty sometimes worked against him. When prospective customers asked, "How much did you pay for this?" he always gave them a truthful answer.

Inevitably the person would then say, "If you only paid that much for it, why should you charge me this much?"

Uncle William would say, "I guess you're right."

In his case, it really did work against him.

Although he may have lacked wisdom, he committed himself to total honesty. I will also note that for a man with no formal education and limited financial resources, he nevertheless built himself a beautiful home, made a good living, and actually did establish a good business. In addition, he devoted himself to providing for the care of a handicapped brother. I believe that many of the good things that Uncle William received came about because he dealt honestly.

Honesty—an absolutely essential ingredient of character if we are going to live by the motto of Think Big.

H = HONESTY

I constantly encounter individuals who believe that they can get away with "just a little" indiscretion. A little—leads to large. And a few—leads to many.

Consider the national scandals in America during the past twenty years. Had any of these individuals been honest, their futures might have been different:

— Richard Nixon, who will go down in history as the only American president forced out of the White House.
— Jim Bakker, who established a multimillion-dollar religious TV ministry but ended up with a forty-year prison sentence.

We can also point to Senator John Tower, who denied drinking and womanizing to Congress, and to presidential hopeful, Gary Hart, who got caught on his boat in conduct unbecoming a senator of the United States.

These individuals were going places in a big hurry. One dark night the skeletons that they had carefully hidden in an obscure closet appeared, grabbed them around the throat, and strangled them. To sum it up: They were dishonest.

If we make a conscious decision from the outset to be honest, decent, clean, and not put skeletons in our closets, then we can concentrate on what we are doing. We will not have to worry about a knock on our door in the middle of the night, a telephone call, or a press conference that tells the world about our indiscretions.

When I talk to young people, I urge them, "Tell the truth. If you tell the truth all the time you don't have to worry three months down the line about what you said three months earlier. Truth is always the truth. You won't have to complicate your life by trying to cover up."

There are four points I want to make about honesty:

1. *When we act dishonestly, we cheat ourselves.* My classmate at Yale found that out—at least I hope he did.
2. *If we are dishonest, we cannot hide it for long.* Amazingly, most of us have an uncanny ability to detect dishonest people. We may have no evidence or hard facts, but we know they are not sincere.

Iraq's Sadaam Hussein, for example, illustrates these points. Dishonest during the crisis in Kuwait, he stated only days before invading Kuwait that he had no intention of invading Kuwait. Subsequent investigations revealed large amounts of monies he was stashing away for himself from the oil revenues of his country. Consequently, his dishonest dealings wreaked havoc and destruction upon his own country.

Furthermore, it was impossible for him to continue to deceive the public, because his intentions became clear once his military aggression started, preventing him from hiding his dishonest intentions. By his actions, Hussein placed himself in a position where no one trusts him and where no one is likely to deal with him in good faith. In short, Saddam Hussein has *earned* the distrust and disdain of the world.

No matter how important, how renowned, or how powerful they become, individuals can still be destroyed by dishonesty.

3. *Dishonest people get treated dishonestly.* Maybe there is a universal law that says that if we treat others deceitfully, we ourselves will get taken in by deceitful individuals.

   Or, to state the golden rule as a biblical principle: "In everything, do to others what you would have them do to you" (Matthew 7:12).

4. *Honest thinkers can Think Big; dishonest thinkers are small-minded.* Their dishonesty may take the form of grand ideas or come up with revolutionary concepts, but their dishonesty makes them self-centered. By being honest with ourselves and with others, we move into that realm of Thinking Big because we not only want good things for ourselves, but for others as well.

In discussing honesty, I think of a couple I met in California—Cliff and Freddie Harris, who organized and still run an outreach program called DAP (Drug Alternative Program).

Cliff had been convicted of a number of crimes, most of them stemming from his addiction to heroin and cocaine, and spent several years behind bars. One day Cliff faced up to his violent, crime-filled life. He became honest with himself and with society.

Now Cliff is trying to help others to live upright and open lives. He and his wife, Freddie, tell young people from their own experience how empty and destructive life can be, and especially about the hopelessness and pain of living in a drug-infested environment.

The quality that most impresses me about Cliff is his utter honesty. Some may call that vulnerability or openness. As he will tell you, Cliff has nothing to hide. He tells anyone who will listen what drugs and crime did to his life. Once he faced himself, Cliff committed himself to help others avoid the mistakes he himself has made. For those already into drugs, he stands ready to show them the way out.

When I talked with Cliff, I remember his saying, "People are simply not willing to look at their problems honestly and admit that they have problems."

I went to one of the Harrises' programs and listened to the testimony of a husband and wife. They said, "We went to church every week. We participated in all the activities, but as soon as we got home, we headed for the bedroom and started popping speed."

They described the destruction that this had brought to their lives, and particularly, what it had done to their teenage daughter. What had begun with an unwillingness to face problems (dishonesty), became a demonic monster that controlled their lives.

Fortunately, they got involved with Cliff and Freddie Harris. In the beginning, the Harrises had to pressure them to admit that they had problems they couldn't cope with—problems they were masking with drugs.

"It wasn't just a little difficulty or a temporary matter. Drugs *controlled* our lives," said the wife.

Finally they got involved in the Drug Alternative Program and were subsequently able to shed these drug habits and to get their family back together.

As soon as the couple stopped speaking, their sobbing daughter came up to the platform. When she finally calmed down, she told us that after seeing their hypocritical lifestyle and knowing her parents' drug habits, "I lost all respect for them. I felt so abandoned, like I was an orphan." Then she smiled and hugged them both. "I'm so happy to have my parents back."

The key to resolving the family conflict in this situation is the willingness to deal honestly with the situation—any situation. Although we all make mistakes in life, the problems occur when we try to hide our mistakes, to cover them up rather than to learn from them and allow other people to learn from them. We have to learn to deal honestly with them.

When we are confronted by failure and mistakes, we can leave them behind and go on with our lives.

H = HONESTY

IF WE LIVE BY THE RULE OF HONESTY
AND ACCEPT OUR PROBLEMS,
WE CAN GO FAR DOWN THE ROAD
OF ACHIEVEMENT.

Nine

Insightful Thoughts

> *No one can make us feel inferior without our permission.*
> —*Eleanor Roosevelt*

As previously confided, when I was growing up, my mother worked in the homes of many wealthy families, sometimes three or four in tandem. Because of her lack of education and training, she did menial and unskilled jobs, such as cleaning homes and baby-sitting, none of which sound like much of a job.

My mother, however, considered every employment opportunity as far more than a job. She decided that wherever she worked, they would say, "Sonya Carson is the best worker we ever had."

While giving them her best, Mother was constantly trying to figure how these people became successful. She also wanted to know how they lived once they were successful. As she went about her work, Mother asked questions and noticed what they read, how they spent their free time, and the kinds of friends and activities they chose.

After a time, she gained invaluable *insight*—an understanding of what made the wealthy people among whom she worked different from the poor people among whom she lived. One thing that she immediately sensed was their attitude toward television. Although they owned TV sets—sometimes as many as five or six—they did not watch the tube much. Instead, they spent a large amount of their time reading and analyzing materials.

Mother also gained insight from observing their clothes. It did not take her long to realize that they selected clothing for its quality, not its faddishness, fashion, or price. "You get what you pay for," Mother said to me several times. She had heard those words from her employers, and she realized they meant it. Often they paid a little higher price for clothes than less affluent people pay, but they got more wear from the material.

Mother understood this, especially during those first years after we returned to Detroit. Mother couldn't afford to buy many new clothes, but that did not stop her from getting us durable goods. Mother didn't seem discomfited to shop at Good Will stores, although I was embarrassed when she took me along, afraid that my school friends would see me there. Mother learned to pick out clothing that breathed quality. Sometimes she had to make alterations on the sewing machine, but when we put them on, we had clothing of eminently higher value than most of what our neighbors wore.

On Deacon Street where we lived, it was not unusual for some of the people we knew to buy expensive clothes (not necessarily quality items) at the better stores. They paid dearly, and often the clothes wore out in a few months.

Because of Mother's insightful attitude, we were able to live on a truly shoestring budget. No one in the neighborhood knew how poor we were because my mother didn't tell them anything about our finances. "They can wonder all they want," she said once. She learned to stretch everything to at least twice its value. Yet, all around us we saw waste.

This ability also had its downside because of the gossip of some of the families who lived near us. A few of them were sure that Mother must be selling her body somewhere; others hinted she was dealing drugs.

"How else can they live so good?" I overheard many times. "That woman's involved in something, you can believe that."

Within five years after our return to Detroit, Mother managed so well that she bought a new car. She was still "just" a domestic worker.

"How are you able to do that?" a neighbor asked as she admired Mother's Chrysler.

Mother, not one to let neighbors intimidate her, gave her usual vague answer. "Easy. I just went right down to the showroom and paid cash, and they sold me the car."

"Is that *another* new dress?" I recall hearing the same woman ask on a different occasion.

"It sure is," Mother said as she walked on. She turned to me and added with a little laugh, "It's certainly new to me." I knew she had bought it at the Good Will store and then spent most of one evening remaking it.

I have repeated details here because I admire my mother. Although she did not even have the chance to finish elementary school, married when she was only thirteen, and her husband whisked her from her native Tennessee to Detroit, Mother never allowed that to hold her back.

She simply used the ability God gave her. For her, at the time when she was almost a nonreader, insight came from observing others, asking questions, and thinking through the answers.

❖   ❖   ❖   ❖

Another example of Mother's insight is in order. By the time I entered tenth grade, I had fallen under the influence of peer pressure. Aside from my schoolwork going downhill for most of one semester, the chief result was that I had to have the kind of clothes that those in my peer group wore. In those days the popular style was anything Italian or leather—especially Italian knit shirts, pants, and a leather jacket. Most also wore the stingy-brim hats.

Because all the members of my peer group had these things, I had to have them as well. "Please, Mother," I remember begging, "please buy me just one outfit. I don't like being different from my friends."

"If they're really your friends, it won't matter how you're dressed."

"But, Mother, you don't understand. *Everybody* dresses that way." I'd name four or five of my friends who came from poorer homes than ours.

Although her answers varied, ultimately she would say, "We don't have the money."

"But I've got to have those Italian knit shirts. Everybody else has them."

"We're not like everybody else."

"But, they're the most important things in the world to me," I said. "I don't want a slew of them. Just a few. Just one outfit."

Exasperated, Mother would finally tell me to be quiet. I knew it wouldn't do any good to say anything more. I sulked a little, then the next night I'd be at her again.

By the time I was into the clothes fad, my grades had fallen precipitously from A to B and I was quickly heading toward being a C student. School didn't matter much; the right clothes, hanging out with these guys, and playing basketball mattered.

One day I really stayed at her by begging for "just one Italian-knit shirt."

Mother sighed deeply before she said, "Benjamin, I'll tell you what. I'm going to turn the budget over to you. You pay for the food and take care of all the other bills. You can have what's left over. I'll bring home every penny in cash and turn it over to you."

"All right! Now you're talking."

"But first, you have to pay the bills," she said. "You count out all the cash I give you and then allocate money for all our basic needs. Put everything down here on the table in piles and mark what it's for. Got that?"

"When do I start? I am ready now!"

"You start Monday morning. Remember, after you pay all the bills, whatever is left, you can have. You can take every penny, every dime, and go downtown and buy all the Italian knit shirts you want."

At last I had won. No more nagging. No more begging for Italian knits and leather jackets. I could buy them myself.

On Monday morning, as she promised, Mother handed me all the money she had made the previous week. Then she handed me a list of expenses for things such as food, gas for the car, and utility bills. Eagerly I worked, allocating the money. Of course, long before I came to clothing I had run out of money.

"There isn't any more money left," I said as I looked up at her. I felt really dejected. All the money was gone and I still hadn't put any money down for lunches or the telephone bill.

"That's right, Bennie. And you know I didn't hold anything back. This is about the same amount I bring in every week."

"I know that," I said. As I looked up at her, for the first time, I felt ashamed for my insistence on Italian knits. "But . . . how do you do it?" I asked.

"Only with the Lord's help," she said.

That was a moment of insight for me. For the first time in my life I truly grasped the meaning of the hardship my mother lived under. No matter how often I looked at the income and compared it with what we had to pay out, it amazed me that my mother had kept Curtis and me alive. And she did it with such style that our neighbors were convinced that we were financially well off.

"You must be a financial wizard," I said.

"With God advising me," she said and laughed, "I sure am!"

Never again did I ask her for an Italian shirt.

The insight carried even further. When I realized how much she did with so little, I also began to think of the other things she had been saying to me for as long as I could remember. If she was able to manage what she had on that budget, maybe some of the other things she was telling me were true, too.

One way to regard this experience is to note that my mother

gained insight through her observations and experiences in the working world. When she applied her insight, it became wisdom.

This much I know for certain: Mother's wisdom rescued me from what might have been another disaster in my life.

❖   ❖   ❖   ❖

When I think about insight, I like to mention my friend, Walter Lomax, a physician in the Philadelphia area. Walter, a millionaire who started from nothing, has a long list of achievements. He owns and operates seven clinics. His five children, whom he raised to be responsible and honest individuals, now run the clinics; therefore, he does not have to worry about dishonesty, pilferage, and embezzlement. Having their support is also one of the reasons he has been able to go so far so quickly.

Beyond the fine work he does in his clinics and in the medical field, Walter has amazing insight into how business works. He is a consultant for many businesses and government agencies because Walter just seems to know what is necessary to attract people to a business, how to treat customers, and how to make them feel important. Walter has achieved what few people could ever achieve in private practice.

Walter combines the qualities of being extremely able and hardworking, which some might call intuition—but that's all right, because it's just a necessary quality for giving one's best.

I = INSIGHT

One way to explain insight is to tell you about the work of Herman Helmholtz. A hundred years ago this German physiologist and physicist described his scientific discoveries by saying that he went through three stages:

1. *Saturation*

   He conducted research, finding out everything he could learn on the subject.

2. *Incubation*

   This is the reflective time, the thinking and mulling over what he learned through research.

3. *Illumination*

   Helmholtz faithfully gave his full concentration to saturation and incubation. Then, he said, he arrived at a *sudden* solution.

Years later, a French mathematician, Henry Poincaré, added a fourth stage, which he called *Verification*. Today we might think of this as proving it, checking it out, and making sure our insight is correct.

❖ ❖ ❖ ❖

Insight works in many ways. It does not have to happen in an instantaneous, magical moment. It can also be a quality that we nurture and develop. Because some people unconsciously lean on their own insight, they sometimes are unaware that they possess it.

Insight occurs at the stage wherein we cry out, "Aha!" or "Eureka!" (which literally means, "I've found it"). Insight enters through many doors, such as when we:

— listen to those who have already achieved, and think that we can do likewise.

— understand that achievement does not just happen to a few, selected people.

— take advantage of the opportunities to learn from any source that can teach us.

— learn from the mistakes (as well as achievements) of others.

In the previous chapter I urge individuals to look at themselves, to think of what they have done well in the past, and to consider what they like to do—all part of the Saturation and Incubation, out of which can come insight.

❖ ❖ ❖ ❖

The events leading to the separation of the Bender Siamese twins are a good example of how insight is obtained. Long before that event, I had been fascinated by the concept of Siamese twins joined at the back of the head and I had spent a great deal of time reading about the various historic attempts at surgical separation of Siamese twins joined at the head.

In looking over the past attempts to separate them (all of them had failed), it became clear to me that the major problem was *exsanguination,* or bleeding to death. After talking to cardiovascular surgeons and reading up on some of the techniques they used, such as hyperthermic arrest (where the body is cooled until the heart stops and the blood is pumped out, at which time they operate on the heart), I had one of those "Aha!" experiences. The insight struck me that we might use such a technique combined with complex cranial facial surgery and vascular reconstruction to eliminate or greatly reduce the risk of exsanguination during the most delicate parts of such separations.

Although I did not know anything about the Binder Siamese twins at the time, this insight obviously played a major role in my career development when the opportunity presented itself.

❖ ❖ ❖ ❖

For me the most important and regular source of insight comes from the book of Proverbs. Anyone familiar with the story of Solomon knows that he made many mistakes in his life—

especially as he grew older. Yet, he was willing to reveal those mistakes to others by writing many proverbs. By heeding his words, we can avoid the same traps.

Although I believe in consulting with and learning from experts and achievers, consultation cannot replace personal preparation. In my opinion, the base of personal preparation comes more from reading than from any other source. That some people do not like to read much is really no substantive argument. The more we read, the better we read and the more we *enjoy* reading. We cannot read too much—and most of us do not read enough.

Foremost of my priorities, as I constantly point out, is the reading of the book of Proverbs. I suggest reading and *rereading* Proverbs, together with the entire Bible, and other good books.

After reading comes the crucial step—reflection. We have to think about what we have read. We make choices, we do certain things because we have thought them out.

For any of us who want a better quality of life there are things we can do. We can go to someone we consider successful who has already reached some of the goals we are striving for, which is particularly important when we observe people whose backgrounds are similar to our own.

We can ask them questions, such as:

— What brought you to where you are now?
— Who are the people who helped the most?
— Who or what almost held you back?
— What did you do that you now wish that you had not done?

We also need to recognize that we have as worthy minds as those whom we consider to be successful. Some insightful ideals that achievers in life have accomplished are that:

— They decided (even if not premeditatively) that they were going to use their ability and their minds to achieve.

— They observed and asked questions.

— They figured out how to work more intelligently by devising easier methods or cutting out wasted effort.

All of us can learn from others. If nothing else, we can prepare ourselves and avoid repeating mistakes. People who tend to achieve little are frequently those who must make all the mistakes for themselves, then spend so much time extricating themselves from their problems that they don't have the energy or the know-how to move forward in the game of life. It gives us a significant advantage if we learn to benefit from the experience of others.

In my medical undertakings, especially controversial ones like the Binder twins' surgery, I have made it a habit to do four significant things:

1. Question the feasibility, the importance, and the need for any new activity. I have to feel that it is a cause that is worth the time and effort required.

2. Talk extensively with more experienced neurosurgeons. Dr. Don Long is one whom I frequently consult. Aside from the fact that he is head of my department, I go to him because he is an experienced and extremely skilled neurosurgeon.

3. Read accounts of neurosurgical adventures and misadventures. This means consulting journals and keeping up with the latest research.

4. Evaluate my options from the gleaned information to help me make my decision.

I could have tried another tactic and said to those who want to help, "Just leave me alone and let me do enough of these surgeries until I have learned from my own mistakes. After that I'll know what I ought to do and what I should avoid." Unfortunately, many patients would have suffered, perhaps even died, from such a trial-and-error method.

Also, I would not have been able to do nearly as much as quickly, because I would have ignored the work of those who had started out ahead of me. This attitude applies to any field, not just medicine.

I can recall a number of people who automatically learned from others and gained insight (which also means *understanding*). They understand why something works or how it functions. By contrast, there are those who only seem to know. We have all met that type—know-it-alls in our society who appoint themselves as infallible experts, but who actually know very little.

Jim Smith is an insightful individual, who hosts two TV programs in the Philadelphia area. When visiting in the Washington-Baltimore area in 1985, he saw me interviewed on TV when I explained hemispherectomies. At the time, we had done only a handful, but they were successful.

As Jim later told me, he was impressed with what he heard and saw and was fascinated with the concept of being able to remove half of a person's brain to cure intractable seizures. To Jim, the surgery was mind-boggling. He invited me to come to Philadelphia so that he could interview me. We did a couple of TV programs, but our relationship did not end there.

Jim arranged for me to meet several people in the Philadelphia educational system and to speak to numerous students in an attempt to get them to Think Big. We have also become good friends with great interest in each other's careers.

A man with an insatiable curiosity, Jim Smith also has an uncanny insight for recognizing something that will benefit others. He then uses his ability to integrate the information into the realm of public awareness. For Jim, the surgeries I performed were not only nice human interest stories about people who had been helped. They were, he recognized immediately, surgeries that could save lives and eventually lead to even more remarkable innovations. Because of that insightful understanding, in every way he knew how, Jim spread the word about this medical breakthrough—the hemispherectomy.

Jim Smith gained insight in a number of areas because he did the right things, beginning with asking questions. Then he spoke with someone he considered an authority—in this case, me. After that, he researched, learned everything he could, and used that information to make the public aware of what was happening with new medical techniques.

Through his contacts, Jim has also opened the door for me to visit several school systems, thus putting me in contact with influential educators and giving me the opportunity to speak to students about concepts important to me.

❖   ❖   ❖   ❖

Most of the successful people I know are either naturally keen observers, or they develop that ability. If they conduct research, they know what to watch carefully. They reflect by asking questions or trying to figure out what might happen. I can apply this same principle to those who work directly with people. Regardless of their field, those who Think Big have this quality in common: They observe the environment around them, whether people or materials.

This is actually what we call the scientific method, which is based on observation. To start with, they may not know anything, but they observe what happens in an experimental process. They scrutinize it time and time again until they see relationships developing. After a while they begin to know that when certain things happen, they can expect specific results. Each piece of scientific knowledge becomes a building block to acquire more details and to develop more sophisticated knowledge.

We could start with observing a single cell, or the components of that cell. If we stay at it and observe long enough, we can begin to understand how our researchers developed insight into DNA and the whole genetic structure. All of these concepts and theories have been built around "reflected observations" that eventually result in insight. I am not implying that everyone should become a scientist, but I do point out that when we strive to acquire the right building blocks and reflect on what we are observing, insight follows.

❖   ❖   ❖   ❖

Moving from the scientific realm, two of the most insightful people I know are my mother and my physician's assistant, Carol James. They both have the ability to look at complex situations and quickly extract what is important. They are especially excellent in human situations.

Although these two might not be conscious of their scientific exercise of reflective observation, both of them have practiced it over a period of years. Even though they cannot explain their insight in steps one through four, they still have the ability to observe demeanor and reactions and to ascertain quickly and accurately people's emotional states. Sometimes the emotional state is obvious, such as when individuals are shouting or crying, but they also pick up more subtle shades of human behavior.

For example, my mother is an expert at identifying a scam. If a person is attempting to sell something by making claims that are untrue, she zeros in.

A vacuum salesman once came by and tried to sell his product. Although she liked his brand, the asking price was outrageous. He insisted, "This is the most powerful vacuum cleaner in its league." He went on with irrelevant claims about how outstanding his product was.

"Very interesting," she said, "but if it's the best in its league, what are other vacuum cleaners doing in the same league?"

"Well," he said, beaming as he gently rubbed his machine, "actually, there aren't any others in this particular league. This one is unique and—"

"So you mean there's nothing on the market anything like your cleaner? Nothing even similar?"

"There are other vacuums, of course—"

"How different is this one? I mean, don't they all do about the same thing?"

"Well, essentially, yes, but—"

She kept the man talking, answering questions, and making admissions. Finally she asked, "But isn't it true that the other brands can do the same things?"

Mother ended up buying the same vacuum cleaner—elsewhere—and at an extremely good price.

Flowing out of her ability to observe, reflect, and then act, Mother has the ability to get people to open up, to get them to tell her the truth about what they are saying.

Carol James, however, has the ability to see that people are angry, even when they demonstrate no outward signs. To people who were seething inwardly, I've heard her say, "I know you must be quite upset. You have the right to feel angry." Such a little statement helps greatly, even if most of us in the same room cannot discern any reaction.

Carol's ability really shines in explaining medical terminology and procedures. When we sit down with families or patients, we try to explain everything. Having no idea how much knowledge or understanding the patients and their families actually have, we do the best we can.

When I start to explain and they do not fully understand something, they may act as if they do comprehend.

"Oh, yes, oh, yes," they say, and even nod their heads. By their responses, I can't always be sure.

Carol knows when they understand, or when they're just not able to say, "I'm confused." After I have finished what I thought was a clear and direct explanation, she has gone back and spoken with the same people—*for another hour.* When she leaves, they really do know what I meant, because she can break everything down into simple language.

Primarily, Carol's ability has come from being a lifelong people watcher. Everyone is not a people watcher; everyone is not a keen observer of scientific data. We all have talents and limitations. We do not need to compare ourselves with others and think that because we are a nurse, or a lawyer, or a garbage collector, that we are either better or worse than a salesperson, a technician, or a librarian.

We need to say, "This is what I am, and as a professional or occupational person, I will do my work extremely well. I am good at what I do. I make people's lives better because of the work I do." This attitude determines whether we are successful—not the amount of money we make or the prestige our title carries.

❖   ❖   ❖   ❖

Last but not least is another insightful friend, Roger Bennett. In his forties, he is a senior partner in one of the major law firms in Baltimore. His honesty is actually what led to our becoming friends. Roger deals with all types of legal problems from business law to personal injury to taxes and estates—and he is good at everything in which he gets involved.

Roger constantly amazes me by his adroitness in analyzing a person's intentions. Because of having seen the results of his lightning-like responses, I have come to have confidence in his insight and understanding of people.

More than once I have discussed people and business ventures with him. Roger has listened and then said, as if pulling his answer out of the air, "This is what they're really after. This is the reason they're presenting it in this fashion."

Or he'll look at another proposal and say, "This is good. I think it's an honest firm, and the program they are presenting is stellar. Take advantage of it."

It is invaluable to know people who have that kind of insight. Roger grew up in a poor, Jewish section of Brooklyn. He had to learn to cope with people, to understand how others think, and to get inside their heads—one of the major reasons he has been able to raise himself from a poverty-stricken environment to a senior partner in a major law firm.

Through my own story and by acquainting others with Roger Bennett, I want to make it clear that having been born on the wrong side of the tracks does not mean that that birthplace has to remain a permanent address. *It is not where we have come from but where we are going that counts!*

By using our talents, by being honest, and by taking advantage of our insights, we can give our best to whatever area of life we want to invest ourselves in—and Think Big. Insight is one of the crucial characteristics that we can develop.

I = INSIGHT

IF WE OBSERVE AND REFLECT
AND COMMIT OURSELVES TO
GIVING OUR BEST,
WE WILL COME OUT ON TOP.

Ten

Nice Guys Finish

So many gods, so many creeds,
So many paths that wind and wind,
When just the art of being kind
Is all this sad world needs.
—Ella Wheeler Wilcox

Nice guys finish last," goes the old saying, especially in the business world. It is another cynical way to reinforce the idea that each of us takes care of ourselves and forgets everyone else. I just don't agree with the evaluation. In fact, in my acrostic for Think Big,

N = NICE

When speaking about *nice,* I use the word as an umbrella to cover a wide range of meaning, including:

thoughtful	considerate	helpful
pleasant	agreeable	gentle
polite	congenial	caring

I have known a number of nice people in my life who have done extremely well, some of whom I have mentioned already in this book: Dr. Don Long, Dr. Mike Johns, and Dr. Walter Lomax.

From my mother I learned about being nice to other people—regardless of who they are or what they have achieved (or haven't achieved!). Mother used to say, "Be nice to everybody. You meet the same people going up as you meet going down."

Although I had learned it earlier, the message really got through to me when I was doing my residency at Hopkins. During those months, I spent up to one hundred twenty hours a week in the hospital, some of them, of course, voluntarily. Most frequently when I was there in the middle of the night unless we had emergencies, the only people to talk to were the cleaning people, clerks, nurses, and nurses' aides. Besides just idly chatting, I realized that many of them had more interesting lives than mine (which consisted of practically living in the hospital).

One of the janitors played in a softball league and had an endless array of intriguing stories about the pennant races. These often-unapplauded people had families and children and aspirations for them just as I knew I would when I had children of my own.

One particular night, after I had enjoyed a really good conversation with the janitor, a cleaning woman, and two nurses' aides, I reflected on the evening. *Being a doctor at Johns Hopkins does not make me any better in God's sight than the individual who has not had the opportunity to gain such an education but who still works hard.*

Perhaps that was not an outstanding insight, but that realization had an impact on me that I hope I never forget.

Of course, I acquired most of this insight at home from my mother—a woman of integrity coupled with great determination and a strong sense of self-worth. That night, after the conversation with the hospital workers, I wondered how others would have reacted to my mother if they had seen her but not known who she is. I wondered, *if she had been working as a cleaning woman in the hospital, how many of them would have stopped to say to her, "What a wonderful woman you are"?*

Or would they have passed her by?

I have watched people react to waiters, secretaries, and receptionists, and who, afterward, despite identifying nametags and signs on those workers' desks, could not tell anyone anything about these people whom they considered just invisible, anonymous beings—individuals not worth knowing.

I am glad that I learned differently. Mother worked with Curtis and me, teaching us not to prejudge others—not to decide on their value before we knew them. She stressed treating everyone with kindness and giving every person a chance.

As surgeons, if we do not consider all other workers as having value and as worth knowing—we are prejudiced, against which the Bible speaks strongly:

> My brothers and sisters, do you with your acts of favoritism really believe in our glorious Lord Jesus Christ? For if a person with gold rings and in fine clothes comes into your assembly, and if a poor person in dirty clothes also comes in, and if you take notice of the one wearing the fine clothes and say, "Have a seat here, please," while to the one who is poor you say, "Stand there," or "Sit at my feet," have you not made distinctions among yourselves, and become judges with evil thoughts? (James 2:1–4 NRSV).

If they had an opportunity to talk with her, the same people who might reject my mother without knowing who she is, might discover (to their amazement) that she is a highly intelligent person with deep insight, extremely knowledgeable for the amount of education she possesses, and someone who might even be able to help them with their problems.

Why can't a janitor know significantly more about certain situations than a neurosurgeon does? A person who performs manual labor can certainly be as intelligent as one who sits at a desk, performing clerical work.

Being nice translates to accepting each person for his or her individual worth. It disturbs me that some still decide that certain people are not worth bothering with simply because of their socio-economic class, job title, or national origin. *Everyone has value.* Or, as a popular saying of my growing-up years reminds: "God don't make no junk."

These under-recognized people can teach us, encourage us, and even be important allies for us. Over the years, I have gotten to know a great number of such people whom I still know and talk with often. When I am in the midst of a group of doctors and a clerk comes by to say hello, I want that individual to be treated just as well as the CEO of an important company who comes in as a patient. Medical-assistance patients are as important as wealthy patients are. All of them have medical needs that we can minister to. Unfortunately, much of the health care system in our country is a class system—those who don't have money do not usually get the best care.

❖   ❖   ❖   ❖

One of the nicest individuals I have ever met is an Australian, Dr. Lynn Behrens, president of Loma Linda University. She started out as a pediatrician, became dean of the medical school, and is now president of the university. She is the most pleasant, down-to-earth, nice person I know. Still only in her early forties, part of the underlying reason for Dr. Behrens' rise to the university presidency has to be her genuine, caring warmth for everyone.

Her husband, Dave Basaraba, is equally nice. An example of a person who has made significant achievements in the field of education, he does not, as the man in the family, feel a need to try to steal the spotlight from his popular wife.

It amazed me to meet such modestly humble and nice people. They have achieved incredible things in a short period of time, a proof that it is not true that one has to be nasty to be successful.

I met Lynn for the first time at my church, when she was with a group of other individuals from Loma Linda School of Medicine.

The only person among them that I knew was the chief of surgery. We had invited the entire group home for dinner after church. That included Lynn, who mixed freely with the others. We had been together for some time sharing a meal before this very nice and modest woman even made it known that she is a doctor—in fact, dean of the school of medicine (which we learned only through a statement by one of the other guests, who mentioned it near the end of the meal).

In that her mannerisms never indicated that she holds such a prestigious position, we could well have spent the whole day with her and left still unaware of the significant achievements in her life.

❖ ❖ ❖ ❖

Because I have an overwhelming number of cases, I am constantly pondering some of the goals that I need to accomplish in the hospital. To fulfill these goals effectively requires the cooperation of many others. I believe that if I had not been nice to these others through the years—when I did not need their help— they would not give their best when I finally do need them.

Being nice always comes back to repay us in the long run.

Once I became an intern and junior resident, I realized that I was entering a different phase of my life. By then, behind my name I had an impressive degree for which I had worked hard. Through the years I have observed a few individuals with an M.D. or a Ph.D. attached to their names, who give the impression that they have been elevated above the masses and divinely placed in a superior category.

I remember that as a first-year medical student we had a professor of physiology who claimed to be among the one thousand smartest people in the world. He believed there is clearly such a mortal as a superior human being—and that he is one of them. He was extremely condescending, particularly to minority students, and although he presented himself as a great man, most of us looked upon him as a buffoon. He was also a lousy teacher.

Unfortunately, sometimes other people feel superior to others and treat specific classes of others as being little more than human. Especially I have noticed that this happens to some individuals as soon as they can append Ph.D. or M.D. after their names. In their mind it is as if the degree or title elevates them above others. Yet, no matter how famous they become or how much they achieve, we do well to remember that they are still the same people they were before they had the degree after their name.

After earning my M.D. degree, I tried to be aware that I was the same person that I had *always* been. Now that I am a board-certified neurosurgeon, I am still the same individual that I was in high school. A man who had trouble learning how to study in college, I am no different now that I have six honorary doctorate degrees. None of these degrees make me any different from the person I was while growing up in the inner cities of Detroit and Boston—or make me any better than a man who earns his living laying pavement, or a woman who types letters every day. Except for the unique circumstances of my life, I could be doing a different kind of work.

❖　❖　❖　❖

An example of this implicit belief's paying off for me is an incident that happened just before Candy and I left for Australia. Although I didn't know it, two nurses were planning to invite me out for a farewell meal with the intention of getting me alone "to have some fun" with me.

I would never have had any way of knowing in advance what they were plotting but for another nurse who, overhearing them making their plans, came to me. "Ben," she said, "I think you need to know what they intend to do."

Consequently, when the two nurses approached me, I found a way not to accept their invitation.

Now if I had treated rudely the nurse who had overheard the other two, she would not have cared what happened to me. But she did care because she had never been "just" another unimportant, impersonal worker.

❖　❖　❖　❖

Even now, in my capacity as director of pediatric neurosurgery, I still get helpful advice from people and I hope that they will always feel free to make suggestions or talk to me.

For one thing, I do not know what I would do without compassionate nurses and nurses' aides who have developed an intuitive sense about their patients. Those under their care become special to them, and often they anticipate relapses and complications, thus making life easier for me and for the improvement of the sick.

Another vivid memory I have of a caring nurse's intervention on my behalf is that involving a mother who brought to the clinic her hydrocephalitic child, a boy who also had many other medical problems. We had reviewed her case, and I was scheduled to see the child personally.

"Ben," one of the nurses said and called me aside. "I've just noticed who your next patient is. Do you mind if I talk to you about his mother for a minute?"

"Tell me anything you can to help," I said.

This nurse had only recently come to Hopkins from another large hospital to which, she told me, the mother had also taken her child. "I know her, although she probably never paid any attention to me. I don't think you want to get involved with her."

Surprised, I asked her why. Although she was reluctant to say much, she finally told me, "To begin with, she's extremely racist. You could probably cope with that. But everywhere she's been—

and she's hit just about every medical facility around—she has caused an endless number of problems." She explained some of them and added, "Already this morning she's been making statements to other families that she's about to 'rip the mighty Ben Carson from his place in the sky and bring him down to earth.' "

By then I had just about decided that I did not want to get involved with her, and the nurse's final statement erased any existing doubt. "Regardless of the outcome, she is likely to try to bring a lawsuit against you."

I thanked the nurse. When I talked to the mother, I said, "I think it would be better if I turn his care over to someone else. I'm not able to deal with your son at this time."

"You're too good to look at my child? You want a case that will bring you more TV interviews?" She was already starting the attack. "Or maybe it's because we don't have a lot of money." On and on she went.

When she paused, I said quite calmly, "I am not able to spend time with your case. I already have a heavy caseload. I think you need to find another neurosurgeon so that you can get immediate treatment for your child."

"Oh, so you do think you're too good, don't you? You think you're better than I am. You won't take care of my child, but you made us sit out there in that waiting room! Because we're not important enough, we could just keep on sitting out there until you got around to saying you aren't interested!"

I don't recall how long she lashed out at me, but by then it had become absolutely clear that the nurse had given me the right information.

The mother and child finally walked out. Yelling at me as she left, telling me how terrible she considered me, her parting words were that she really hadn't wanted to see me anyway.

The situation did not particularly distress me. Rather, I was feeling grateful to the nurse who had been nice enough to warn me so that I could get myself out of a no-win situation before something serious developed.

Such people can be devastating to a person's career. Not often, but occasionally, such troublemakers do pop up. No matter how helpful we try to be or how much we go out of our way, we will never satisfy them.

That is sad, of course. But to have those people who work beside me and who care enough to seek me out and to inform me— sometimes at no small risk to themselves—only reinforces the *nice* principle once again.

In the acrostic for Think Big, I made N stand for *NICE*. I want to do more than say, "Be nice." Here are a few reasons that we should extend niceness to the people we encounter each day.

1. *Everyone in the world is worth being nice to.* Because God never creates inferior human beings, each person deserves respect and dignity.

2. *We get out of life what we put into it.* The way we treat others is the way we ourselves get treated. When I was a boy, I used to hear the saying, "Pretty is as pretty does." I'd like to change that to "Nice is as nice does."

3. *We don't lose by being nice.* One elderly gentleman once said, "When I treat other people with kindness and love, it is part of my way of paying my debt to God and the world for the privilege of living on this planet."

Even though it is true that some people will take advantage of kindness and might even consider it weakness, in the long run, kindness still prevails.

First Corinthians 13, the famous passage about love, comes to mind. Being nice comes under the meaning of the word *love*. My friends who know theology well tell me that biblical love (Greek, *agape*) is an attitude, an act of the will, a form of behavior, and not an emotion.

Therefore, to paraphrase 1 Corinthians 13:1–3, interchanging for *love* the word *nice:*

> If I speak in the tongues of men and of angels, but am not nice, I am only a resounding gong or a clanging cymbal. If I have the gift of prophecy and can fathom all mysteries and all knowledge, and if I have a faith that can move mountains, but am not nice, I am nothing. If I give all I possess to the poor and surrender my body to the flames, but am not nice, I gain nothing.

N = NICE

IF WE ARE NICE TO OTHERS,
OTHERS RESPOND TO US IN THE SAME WAY,
AND WE CAN GIVE OUR BEST
FOR EACH OTHER.

Eleven

Knowledge Counts

Knowledge is power.
—*Francis Bacon*

O*h, that's not* relevant for today."

"I don't need to know that."

"You're overloading your brain with useless information."

"What good are algebra and chemistry and history going to do me when I am working in sales?"

I have heard all the arguments against learning, and most of them reduce to:

(1) Too much learning overtaxes the brain.

(2) Certain kinds of knowledge are irrelevant.

The first argument is untrue. The second argument mistakenly implies that we need to learn only the material that we will actually use in our jobs.

Neither argument is valid.

Before I refute them, I want to point out that in my acrostic for Think Big, I decided that

K = KNOWLEDGE

This subject is dear to my heart because so often knowledge is disdained, particularly among students in inner-city schools. I am also encountering this attitude in suburban schools where we would ordinarily expect students to thirst for knowledge.

I refute the two general arguments against learning, with the following contentions:

First, we cannot overload the human brain. This divinely

created brain has *fourteen billion* cells. If used to the maximum, this human computer inside our heads could contain all the knowledge of humanity from the beginning of the world to the present and still have room left over.

Second, not only can we not overload our brain—we also know that our brain retains *everything*. I often use a saying that, "The brain acquires everything that we encounter." The difficulty does not come with the input of information, but in getting it out. Sometimes we "file" information randomly, or tie significant bits of information to information of little importance, and it confuses us.

All knowledge is important—a fact that some people do not want to hear. One of the wonderful things about learning is that knowledge not only translates from one area to another but is also an avenue that leads to understanding and insight.

For example, students often complain about the social studies courses as irrelevant, particularly history and geography. What they often do not grasp is that these subjects broaden their mental horizons. History helps us to understand the past—how we got the way we are. Geography explains many customs and events based on the land.

The Persian Gulf War, which for several months was the center of world attention, is now history. Why are the countries of Iraq, Iran, Kuwait, and Saudi Arabia important? I find it surprising that so many young people do not understand that those countries have only one natural resource upon which their entire economy has been built: vast reservoirs of fuel oil that the rest of the world covets.

We might then wonder how oil got in those places? Where else can we find what we call "fossil" fuels? Pursuing such lines of questioning can lead us into new areas of knowledge—and teach us to reason more clearly.

I am convinced that knowledge is *power.*

— To overcome the past—
— To change our own situations—
— To fight new obstacles—
— To make better decisions.

Furthermore, knowledge makes people special. An example that comes to my mind is W. Duncan ("Fred") McCleary, our sons' pediatrician. Fred trained to be a teacher and taught in the elementary schools. In his thirties he decided he would rather be a physician, so he applied to and was accepted by a medical school.

Did Fred waste his training as a teacher? Some might think so. As a parent, however, I am convinced that because of his teacherly love for children, Fred has transferred that skill and information over to his work as a pediatrician. And we, the parents and patients, gain from his vast knowledge.

I've talked with Fred often. I've observed the way he relates to parents and children. First, with no fanfare concerning it, his knowledge of pediatrics is obvious. *He knows his field of work.* Second, and evidence of his educational background, Fred is extremely practical in his approach. When children are around him, he has the caring instinct of an educator tied in with the knowledge of a physician. Even though Fred is not a full-time pediatrician working in a large tertiary medical center (major referral center), his clinical skills certainly equal those of the best academic physicians I know.

Whenever I speak to groups, especially to students, I try to stress the value of knowledge, often revealing a little of my back-ground. One of the particulars I stress is my acquired knowledge of classical music, which, briefly, came about this way: One of the television programs I watched was called *College Bowl.* I loved the quiz program, which asked college students questions ranging from geography and history to science and mathematics. By the time I had reached tenth grade, I was pretty good at knowing the answers. I'd say, "I know those answers. I could go to college and do well." Then I began to dream that I'd enter college and compete on *College Bowl*. *Why not?* I kept asking myself. *I am as smart as they are; I can learn anything they already know.*

However, *College Bowl* had two categories that I was not a whiz at: art and classical music. After all, what would a poor, black kid from a lower economic background in Detroit know about those two areas?

They frequently showed pictures by Van Gogh and Renoir and asked students to identify them. Or they would play a piece of music by Rachmaninoff or Schubert. "Name the piece and the composer."

One day I made a decision to learn just as much about art as any of those *College Bowl* students had. I began going downtown to the Detroit Institute of Arts, at first roaming through the galleries, learning what pictures were there. Then I began reading about the artists, finding out when they painted, the name of each time period, when the artists were born and died, and what terms the art world used to describe their work. Sure, it was work, but it was also fun because I not only learned about art, but my appreciation of art also increased.

From there, I tackled classical music. We had a radio station that played classical music all the time (and identified the selections), so I managed to buy a transistor radio and kept it tuned to that station. My friends thought I was weird. After all, why would a black kid from Motown listen to Mozart?

Not caring what they thought, I knew what I was doing: preparing myself for college. In time, I could identify most of the classical pieces played on *College Bowl*. Even more fun for me, often I could call out the information long before the contestants did.

When I talk about that area of my life, the question I get is, "Yes, but why is it important for me to know about classical music?"

"It's not important to know just about classical music, but to know about all historical forms of music," I say. "It's also good to know about art history. If you're a member of an ethnic or minority group, you need to know about your heritage. Then learn how that fits in with world history in general."

Of course, that is not a full answer to the question, but then I add, "What you need to know is determined by what group you intend to influence."

— If your intention is only to influence those who live in your house, then you only need to know about those things that are important to the people with whom you live.
— If you intend to influence those in your neighborhood, you have to broaden your knowledge ongoing.
— If you intend for your life to make a difference in your city, how can you do so if you don't know what's going on?
— If you want to help shape the nation or the world, you will need still more knowledge and learning about what is significant in national and international scope.

People need to recognize that there is every reason to be proud of their ethnic heritage—that there is no such thing as an inferior race or group. They also need to realize that, regardless of their backgrounds, *everyone forms part of the human family.* If we want to make our lives count for the betterment of the human family, we must acquire every bit of knowledge available to us.

It also seems to me that if we were to commit ourselves to gaining knowledge, it would stop name-calling and resentment and hinder such wailing as

— "They won't let me get ahead."
— "The system only works against people like me."
— "What chance do I have?"

A basic element of my philosophy of life is that *no knowledge is wasted.*

Knowledge enriches life itself. Knowledge makes us better

people. Knowledge broadens our grasp of the world around us.

If, to some, these sound like high-flown claims for knowledge, perhaps the best way I can emphasize the worth of knowledge is to finish my story about classical music. To begin with, I never did appear on the TV program, which, unfortunately, went off the air the same year I entered college. Some significant and practical things did happen to me, however, as a result of my reaching for knowledge.

As I tell in detail in *Gifted Hands,* after graduating from medical school, I went to Johns Hopkins for an interview. It was the number one school on my list because I wanted so earnestly to enter their internship program. It might have been demoralizing had I known that they averaged one hundred twenty-five applications each year for the two positions in the neurosurgery program.

During the interview, Dr. George Udvarhelyi, head of the neurosurgery training program, mentioned that he had heard a concert the night before.

"I heard it, too," I said.

"You did?" Even if I hadn't heard the element of surprise in his voice, I would have seen it from the expression on his face.

We discussed the concert, moved into a discussion of classical music in general, and soon the time allotted for the interview had run out.

I was one of the two interns accepted into the neurosurgery residency program.

Years later, George Udvarhelyi told me that the way I had handled myself in the interview had impressed him. Although we have not talked specifically about the interview, I am convinced that my knowledge of and appreciation for classical music factored in his recommendation.

Another reason that I have always been thankful that I got to know classical music is Lacena Rustin, an incoming student also from Detroit, whom I met just before starting my third year at

Yale. A particularly bright person, she had chosen a double major of pre-med and music. Because of her talent for and my interest in classical music, as well as my ability to play several instruments, we started talking. The more we talked, the more I liked her and wanted to keep on talking.

Four years later, I married Lacena, whom everyone calls Candy.

❖ ❖ ❖ ❖

One day a high school student asked me, "Dr. Carson, why in the world do I need to know about the electric charges placed on a particle as it goes through a force field? This is totally irrelevant to me."

"How do you know? How do you know what you'll be doing fifteen years from now? You may find that knowing how to figure out the force field in a particular area will open a door for you that might otherwise never be opened. You never know how useful even seemingly insignificant knowledge can be."

Aside from the question of relevance, knowledge makes us valuable. When we have knowledge that other people do not readily have, somebody needs us. It does not matter what we look like, or where we came from, if we have something that others have a need for.

Let me tell you about such a person. Early in 1991 I met a young, black, female executive who worked for a Fortune 500 company in the northeast. She had acquired a great deal of knowledge about the company for which she was working. She had become extremely valuable to them because of her efficiency and her general knowledge in their business area.

Then she married a professor at a university in the South. She informed the CEO of the company that she was going to have to resign.

"But we need you," he said.

"I am sorry," she said. "I love working here. You know that. But I love my husband, and he has tenure—"

"Give us a chance to think it over," the CEO said, "and see what we can work out."

She could not foresee that the corporation could work out anything. Her husband taught in Florida—quite a long way from Philadelphia.

A few days later the CEO talked to her again. This woman had made herself so valuable to that large corporation that he said, "If you'll stay with us, we'll buy you another home. You and your husband can own a house in Florida and another in Philadelphia. And, at company expense, we'll provide transportation as often as necessary during the week so you can commute back and forth."

Clearly a company would not make such an offer to someone it did not need. It did not matter that she was female or that she was black. All that mattered was that because of her applied knowledge, she had made herself so valuable that the company felt that it could not do without her.

This is not to say that unfairness, or racism, or sexism do not exist in our society. It is to say that if individuals who are disadvantaged by these unpleasant facts of life can acquire the kind of knowledge that makes them valuable, they certainly will have a significant advantage when it comes to equalizing or augmenting their opportunities.

One of the ideas that I like to impress on minority students is that knowledge is one tool with which to destroy racial prejudice. I tell them, "Knowledge helps you know that you're as good as they are." I also emphasize that learning can help overcome racial prejudice because of the service we can offer. No one *needs* an ignoramus; no one *wants* an ignoramus.

Class and racial prejudices exist and always will exist as long as there are people who are physically, socially, and economically different. We cannot eradicate prejudice, but we can get rid of some of it and certainly help decrease its power.

My mother once told me something that I will never forget: "If you go into an auditorium filled with racist people, you don't have a problem. *They* have a problem because they're all worried about where you're going to sit. They're afraid you're going to sit next to them. But you can sit anywhere you want."

In that simply stated wisdom my mother was telling me several things. Knowledge, she was saying, would set me free from prejudice. I have often thought of the words of Jesus, "Then you will know the truth, and the truth will set you free" (John 8:32).

She was also saying that once knowledge frees me, although others might still have a problem—even if I cannot take away their problems, I can still be free.

"If I obtain knowledge," I told a group of students in a middle school, "develop my talents and achieve, *others* can get an ulcer, have a stroke, or suffer a heart attack because of their emotional burdens, and I can be there at the hospital to take care of them!"

I firmly believe that most people are not innately base-minded but products of their environment and of the teaching they received from school, peers, and their social conditioning. Sometimes it is just a matter of reconditioning and reeducating people.

It's like the old fairy tales about turning a pumpkin into a coach, or of turning a frog back into a prince. We can play a part in performing comparable wonders by freeing ourselves from ignorance. Then we can help others reach for enlightenment.

❖   ❖   ❖   ❖

Conversely, I want to point out that knowledge can have negative results. In his letter to the Corinthians, Paul wrote about a problem in the church. They lived in a time when people offered food to idols. After the religious ceremony, anyone could buy it. Some Christians in Corinth bought the meat because it was obviously first-quality and must have been offered at bargain prices.

Those who bought the secondhand food did so from knowledge—awareness of its previous use—and also awareness that idols are nothing. Others, however, having more tender consciences, said, "That food was dedicated to false gods. Even now if we eat it, we are worshiping those idols."

So the controversy went until Paul settled the matter: "Now about food sacrificed to idols: We know that we all possess knowledge. Knowledge puffs up, but love builds up" (1 Corinthians 8:1).

Paul, the spiritual father of the church at Corinth, came down a little hard on those with their knowledge, saying, in effect, that it is fine to have knowledge, but do not hit others over the head with it. He concluded, "Therefore, if what I eat causes my brother to fall into sin, I will never eat meat again, so that I will not cause him to fall" (1 Corinthians 8:13).

Sometimes our knowledge has that adverse effect—it puffs us up, and we become a little intolerant of others who do not know as much as we do—but that is not the kind of knowledge to which I refer.

In fact, I can tell you from my own experience how terrible this knowledge is. As I have already pointed out, in fifth grade I had no competition for the lowest ranking in my class. Then Mother forced me to start reading and stop my indiscriminate watching of television. My life turned around, as did my grades. I zoomed to the top of the class.

Maybe I was just trying to show off, was overcompensating, or just didn't know any better, but for a couple of years I made sure that everyone knew how knowledgeable I was.

Instead of responding with awe and appreciation, my classmates saw me as obnoxious and overbearing. Unfortunately, they were right.

By contrast, we have all met individuals who just seem to know what they are talking about—not because they boast, and not because they tell you how much they know. It is simply apparent by the way they function. This kind of knowledge gives them an inner confidence. When we are in their presence, they exude self-assurance, and somehow that makes us feel more self-confident.

That competent, self-assured knowledge does not show off, behave obnoxiously as I used to, or make them appear cocky—it's just there.

The best exemplar I can give of such knowledge is Don Long, the chairman of the neurosurgery at Hopkins. Although he would never try to impress anyone with his experience and vast store of knowledge, he really does seem to know everything about neurosurgery. Throughout years of practice, along with his talents, he has gained remarkable insight from knowing the results of what people have done before. He has gleaned from their successes and mistakes and seeks ways to do a better job at Hopkins.

When Don Long talks about something in that deep voice of his, it becomes abundantly clear that he is not just "shucking and jiving." He knows exactly what he's talking about—and all of us listen with respect. We are aware of his credibility and know that he is not trying to impress us with his storehouse of information.

Sometimes I tell students, "Knowledge is the key that unlocks all the doors. You can be green-skinned with yellow polka dots and come from Mars, but if you have knowledge that people need, instead of beating you, they'll beat a path to your door."

❖   ❖   ❖   ❖

In high school I began reading journals like *Psychology Today,* and in college I majored in psychology. Through the years I have learned that our responses and actions are generally based upon our accumulated experience and knowledge, whether or not we recognize it at the time. Consequently, the acquisition of knowledge—any knowledge—is likely to better prepare us for responding to difficult situations in the future.

People sometimes say or do things that seem just right for the situation at hand. Often they are not aware that they base their words or actions on knowledge acquired years earlier—one of the facts that I want to emphasize in saying that "the brain acquires everything that we encounter." When we watch a television program, our brains completely record it. If we listen to a symphony, again our brains take in everything—as they do when we listen to rock-and-roll music. Only upon reflecting and analyzing the situation later do we realize this. In a subsequent chapter is the story of Matthew Thompson. Because I remembered something that I had learned thirteen years earlier, we were able to change the course of his life.

An important verity about knowledge is that *the brain works most effectively with consciously retained information.* We more easily remember what we want to recall later. When we feed our fourteen billion brain cells with information that will enrich us and help others, we are really learning to Think Big.

K = KNOWLEDGE

IF WE MAKE EVERY ATTEMPT
TO INCREASE OUR KNOWLEDGE
IN ORDER TO USE IT FOR HUMAN GOOD,
IT WILL MAKE A DIFFERENCE
IN US AND IN OUR WORLD.

Twelve

Books Are for Reading

*Every man who knows how to read has it
in his power to magnify himself, to
multiply the ways in which he exists,
to make his life full, significant, and
interesting.*

—Aldous Huxley

*H*ow old was Ben Carson when he moved to Boston?"

"What rule did his mother lay down for him and his older brother, Curtis?"

"How old was Dr. Carson when he became the head of the pediatric neurosurgery unit at Johns Hopkins?"

I wonder if you can imagine how I felt when six students came to the stage and began to recite my life and achievements. When they finished, other students threw questions at them, including those above.

No one had warned me that this would happen, so it unfolded as a total surprise. I felt deeply humbled, yet immensely elated. The students at the Old Court Middle School in Baltimore had read every article they could find about my life. This was in 1988, nearly two years before the release of my autobiography, *Gifted Hands.*

Then, just before I spoke, they had another surprise for me.

"Dr. Carson," said one of the students as she read from a paper she had obviously worked hard to compose. As I recall, her words went something like this:

"Here at Old Court Middle School we have formed
the Ben Carson Reading Club. We were so inspired

by your example of reading two books a week and not watching more than two television programs a week that we have formed a club in your name. Each of the members has promised to follow the example that you set for us."

She finished by reading the names of the members. The number of names surprised me.

Several things impressed me: First, that they knew so much about me. Second, that they considered me important enough to glean so much information about me. Third, and what touched me most deeply, that they were looking at me as a role model. For a few seconds I hardly knew what to say. I had no idea that they considered me as influential in their lives.

Just as much of a shock—but a delightful one—was that the students would think of someone who had accomplished things in the intellectual arena in the same spirit that they would rally behind a sports or entertainment personality—traditionally, the only ones considered heroes. That is partially the fault of the media, of course, which has not always acted responsibly in the way it has featured such individuals.

Because these middle school students (grades six through eight) had selected me instead of a sports personality, I kept thinking, *These kids can do something with their lives. They're ready to concentrate on intellectual development instead of getting hung up on rock stars and quarterbacks.*

These kids can go far. They're moving in the right direction because they have learned an important secret that so few others seem to know these days: They are *reading*, and the reading of books opens up worlds of information and possibilities. I am honored to have them name a club after me.

Too, although I have been delighted to find in my travels across the country that many students have started or joined Ben

Carson Clubs in Philadelphia, Texas, and California, it is not important to me to have clubs named after me. It is important, though, to urge young people to read and to stimulate the incredible brain that God gave them at birth.

To join most of these clubs, students have to promise three things:

1. To read two books a week;
2. To submit a report on each book to the club; and
3. To limit time spent in watching television.

Several of the programs are quite successful. They function almost as Alcoholics Anonymous meetings do. Members encourage each other, sometimes offering each other solutions for conquering TV addiction, or tips on how to read more effectively. Because they know the value of educating themselves through their reading, they divorce themselves from frivolous entertainment. Through their own self-determination they are now concentrating on the acquisition of knowledge.

"Dr. Carson, I wanted to tell you what I learned about myself," said one member of a BC Club. "I never thought I could learn so much in such a short time."

"You know what? I am just as smart as anybody else in my class," said an eighth-grade girl. "Because I didn't read well, I just thought I was kind of dumb. Now I know better."

❖ ❖ ❖ ❖

In addition to hearing from a number of Ben Carson reading clubs around the country, I have received information from newspaper clippings, school announcements, and letters that several Ben Carson Scholarship programs have been started.

The most notable of these is at the University of Massachusetts, Boston Campus. I was invited to that university for the inauguration and celebration of a program that provides full scholarships with all expenses paid to minority students from disadvantaged backgrounds, set up especially for those who do not have financial backing. Several students are selected each year to receive these scholarships. Even so, all of them have to demonstrate that they meet academic qualifications for acceptance into the University of Massachusetts.

The uniqueness of this program not only provides financial assistance but offers counseling and social services to ensure that each of the students completes his or her education.

This scholarship was named after me instead of someone long-dead, I was told, to encourage students and to help them realize that it is possible with great determination, hard work, and self-reliance, to overcome seemingly insurmountable odds.

I feel greatly honored by the establishment of this scholarship, particularly because it happened in a city in which we once lived in dire poverty. Boston is also the city where my mother realized that it is possible to make it on her own and not have to be a victim of society.

❖   ❖   ❖   ❖

I received a letter from a family in Arkansas stating that they had read my story and that everyone in the family had been inspired. The mother, who was on public assistance, went back to school and is now pursuing a law degree. Both children had been mediocre students but have now turned their grades from C's, D's, and F's, to A's and B's, but mostly A's. Both are planning to pursue careers in medicine. Countless young people and adults have written to me, or told me when they see me, that my story has had that effect on them. This is just as gratifying to me as successful surgical outcomes.

I am proud of them because they have turned over a new leaf.

They have developed self-confidence and they know that their ability to read well can open any door they choose to go through.

It is chiefly through books that we enjoy intercourse with superior minds.... In the best books, great men talk to us, give us their most precious thoughts, and pour their souls into ours. God be thanked for books. They are the voices of the distant and the dead, and make us heirs of the spiritual life of past ages. Books are true levelers. They give to all, who will faithfully use them, the society, the spiritual presence, of the best and greatest of our race.

—*William Ellery Channing*

In my acrostic for Think Big,

B = BOOKS

Although we can learn in many ways, I am convinced that books are the best source for acquiring knowledge. Here are three significant serendipities that reading furnishes us:

1. Reading activates and exercises the mind.
2. Reading forces the mind to discriminate. From the beginning, readers have to recognize letters printed on the page, make them into words, the words into sentences, and the sentences into concepts.
3. Reading pushes us to use our imagination and makes us more creatively inclined.

Reading actually does activate the mind in the same way that we activate muscles when we lift weights. The more active our minds are, the more agile they become, which results in a higher level of creativity. As someone wisely pointed out, "The mind, once stretched by an idea, never returns to its original dimensions."

Developmental psychologists now estimate that ninety-eight percent of babies are born with creative ability. When we ponder this theory, it makes good sense. What else can infants do all day except lie around and use their imagination? From their first moments of life, babies have needs. They must creatively develop ways of communicating their needs to parents through movements and noise.

These same developmental psychologists estimate, however, that less than five percent of us have remained creative by age eighteen.

"Creative," as used by these psychologists, means using the imagination to come up with innovative ideas, or finding new ways to look at old problems.

It occurs to me that babies do not know what other people have thought about before; they are not limited in their imagination. No one has yet pounded into their thinking that kicking their feet or wiggling their toes will give their parents a message. I am amazed at the creative ways infants find to express their basic need for food or diaper changes.

Fifteen years after birth, however, many of those same clever and creative infants, now teenagers, spend much of their time looking at television or videos. They have images and sounds already packaged and ready for them at the flip of the button. This lifestyle requires them to use little imagination. Why should they? Everything is done *for* them, including telling them how to dress, think, and behave. Consequently, they do not get into the habit of thinking for themselves. All they have to do is follow. Even when we talk about the so-called intellectual programs on television, we might ask, *Are they truly stimulating the intellect?* I have serious reservations.

We can watch a presidential press conference without even having to think about its message or trying to analyze it. Immediately afterward, a network news anchor digests it for us, giving us a blow-by-blow analysis. Usually the first one then pauses so that a second commentator can analyze it some more.

We have gotten away from analyzing matters for ourselves, from thinking ideas through, from creatively using our minds and imaginations. Ultimately, it is costing us. If we scrutinize just the decline of science in this country, we can see that our indifference to creatively using our intellects is going to cost a great deal more in the long run.

Of all the industrialized countries in the world, we are currently dead-last on the list in our students' abilities to understand science and math, partly because we do not start teaching science and math early enough on an in-depth level. Our schools are set up so that we do not get the real material of those subjects until high school. By then, interests have already been developed in other (often trivial) areas.

Just as much at fault, however, is our allowing science to come across as boring and uninvolving. We put too little money into true education, preferring to spend larger and larger amounts on football and basketball. Favorite nonfiction TV fare centers around programs such as *Lifestyles of the Rich and Famous* and *America's Funniest Home Videos,* rather than on *Nova,* or *Jeopardy,* or *Nature.* We find virtually nothing from those who want to make our environment comfortable, provide us with fantastic inventions, add to our knowledge, and encourage research so that we can lead longer and healthier lives.

I am not opposed to popular entertainment. I do, however, at least urge balance. I would like to see authority figures and highly achieving individuals proclaim, *"Read! Read! Read!"* I would like those who have already achieved to show their concern by grabbing others' hands and crying, "Here is the treasure chest of the world—the public library, or a bookstore."

People with high visibility or great influence in our society have a responsibility to improve the society. Such individuals frequently have significant insights concerning the necessary developmental factors involved in success. The acquisition of sound, in-depth knowledge is clearly one of the most important factors that these individuals should feel a responsibility to stress. To do otherwise is not only selfish and irresponsible but unwise, because if they allow the society to deteriorate, *their* offspring will also suffer the consequences.

Because I feel strongly about this, I want to go on record with a strong statement: If we would spend on education half the amount of money that we currently lavish on sports and entertainment, we could provide complete and free education for every student in this country.

The dividends that we would ultimately reap would be phenomenal. America again would quickly rise to preeminence as an intellectual nation. Once again we would be the nation that the rest of the world yearns to imitate in terms of creativity and economic prosperity.

In traveling across the United States and talking with leaders and achievers, I have observed a simple fact about the influence of books. I want to pass this on because of its simplicity and the implications for a generation of American children: *Students who excel academically, read extensively.* I suspect that there is virtually a one-to-one correlation between avid reading and intellectual accomplishments.

As I explain this part of my acrostic for Think Big so that B = Books, I often think of a fellow I met at Yale named Kurt.

Although he was a couple of years ahead of me, I noticed him almost from the time I first got to college.

We had bright students all around us, but Kurt stood out among them. I recall saying to Larry, my roommate, "Keep your eye on him. He's going to be a successful politician one day."

Kurt is black, just under six feet tall, somewhat stocky, clean-shaven, and extremely bright. He wears small, Ben Franklin-type glasses. He was an excellent football player and excelled at everything else he did. After Yale, Kurt became a Rhodes scholar at Oxford, a graduate of Harvard Law School, and a White House Fellow. Kurt always had a following, no matter where he went. People spoke highly of everything that he did.

After Kurt left Yale, I concentrated on my career and lost track of him. A few years later he returned to his hometown of Baltimore and became, at age thirty-six, the state attorney for the city of Baltimore.

By the way, Kurt Schmoke is currently the mayor of Baltimore —and I doubt that he'll stop there.

I admire Kurt tremendously—as I have since I met him nearly twenty years ago. He is probably one of the few mayors with such outstanding educational credentials to head a major United States city.

Another quality I admire about Kurt Schmoke: He pushed the city council to adopt a slogan: BALTIMORE—THE CITY THAT READS.

Kurt himself is a voracious reader and a man of truly outstanding intellectual accomplishments. One message that Kurt Schmoke sends to young people is: "Read. Read books. That's how to get someplace in life."

Kurt is a powerful and living statement, a government official who advertises and pleads for us to read more.

❖   ❖   ❖   ❖

Before I discontinue writing about B = Books, I want to tell you about Harvey and Katherine Wachsman and their family.

I sometimes become involved in legal cases as a legal witness. In one particular case I was defending another neurosurgeon in the Maryland area, who was involved in a significant lawsuit. Dr. Harvey Wachsman was the prosecuting attorney. Both a neurosurgeon and an attorney, he is the president of the American Professional Liability of Lawyers Association. It became very clear during his line of questioning that he has savvy and is extremely clever and knowledgeable.

I have always found that testifying or giving depositions in such cases is fascinating. In every instance, I have adhered to the principle of speaking only the truth. After telling the truth, however, I have no qualms about allowing the opposing side to dig its own grave before I have to speak up and correct them at some point.

This was my first opportunity to see Harvey Wachsman in action. As I have since learned, he frequently approaches his line of questioning with a similar rationale. That is, he allows witnesses to go too far down the wrong path before pointing out the errors or inconsistencies that tend to discredit them.

In one case, we were both aware of what the other was doing and we were having fun, avoiding each other's traps and matching wits. After my deposition was over, we started talking and discovered that we had many common interests. Subsequently our families have become great friends.

Some people might ask, "How can a neurosurgeon and a malpractice lawyer ever be friends?" It turns out that once I got to know this individual, I learned that he does not pursue unmeritorious cases. He spends a great deal of his time and energy pursuing injustice that is not associated with medical practice.

I also learned that he had been active in the civil rights movement and had become involved with some of the struggles in

South Africa. Contrary to some of the negative publicity for his activities, he is an extremely decent person.

Even more impressive is his tremendous library at home. Harvey reads ravenously and knows virtually everything about history. His wife, Katherine, who is also a lawyer, reads widely. Both are extremely knowledgeable, a fact that I discovered the first time we played Trivial Pursuit, a favorite game of mine. The addition of Harvey to my same team makes us unbeatable. An avid reader—especially of history—he is almost impossible to stump.

This thirst for knowledge has been acquired by their five younger children, who are among the best-informed young people I have ever observed. One son, David, is one of the most impressive children I've known in my lifetime. At only age *seven*, David Wachsman is as voracious a reader as his parents.

One day David and I talked about what he wants to do with his life. He said, "I want to be a baseball player, a lawyer, a neurosurgeon, president of the United States, and a writer. And in that order."

That boy might just do all of those things—and in that order. Why not? At age seven, David already knows geography, history, and science better than does the average high school student. He is computer literate. During the summer and on non-school nights, David frequently stays up until midnight, reading. What a child can do when encouraged to move toward the acquisition of knowledge amazes me.

I also want to add that no one pushes him. For David, studying is fun, and he enjoys every minute of it. Quite matter-of-factly he said to me, "If I didn't like doing it, I probably wouldn't do it any more."

Both of David's parents are a source of inspiration to me and many others. Harvey Wachsman has also set an example by being one who started out in life from the lower rungs of the societal ladder. Although now a multimillionaire, Harvey grew up in the

Bedford-Stuyvesant area of New York City—one of the poorest economic sections of the city.

I had not heard of the Wachsman family before Harvey questioned me as a medical expert, so I was surprised to learn that they had independently adopted a reading program similar to the one my mother had put me on in fifth grade.

They allow their children to watch TV infrequently. Before they had even heard of me, the Wachsmans had put their eight children (all of whom are bright) on a program of reading two books a week and submitting a book report.

There is just no limit to what people can accomplish when they develop their minds and use books to acquire knowledge.

B = BOOKS

IF WE COMMIT OURSELVES TO READING
THUS INCREASING OUR KNOWLEDGE,
ONLY GOD LIMITS HOW FAR
WE CAN GO IN THIS WORLD.

Thirteen

In-depth Learning

> *Whatsoever thy hand findeth to do, do it*
> *with thy might.*
>
> —*Ecclesiastes*

Two-year-old Seymour was going down stairs at home when he fell. He hit the bottom and lay sprawled out, unconscious. His frantic parents brought young Seymour to the pediatric ICU at Johns Hopkins. A CAT scan indicated hematomas (blood clots) in both the deep mid-portion of the frontal lobes and in the right temporal lobe.

The physician who first saw Seymour assumed that the hematomas resulted from the boy's fall—a natural assumption. The doctor, using his knowledge and training, was treating the child conservatively.

When I looked at the CAT scan the next day, I commented, "These are strange places for traumatic hematomas. It seems to me they ought to be a little more anteriorly placed (a little farther forward on the brain)."

The other two surgeons present did not seem to think that significant when I brought up the idea. One said, "We think the position of the hematomas is appropriate for the traumatic insult."

That might have been the final diagnosis, except that I had reservations. Although I couldn't pinpoint a medical text I had read, something I had once learned nagged at me. The feeling remained fairly strong that Seymour's problem was more than two aneurysms, as serious as they were. Unable to shake the feeling, I finally said, "I think this child ought to undergo an angiogram to look at the blood vessels in the head."

"You honestly think so?" asked one of the other doctors. His puzzled expression showed me he didn't understand.

"I wouldn't be surprised if we discover that this child has some underlying vascular malformation that caused the bleeding."

"You mean that something else caused the fall, rather than the fall having caused the bleeding?"

I nodded. "I am not sure why, but I feel strongly about it."

After more discussion, they agreed that I might be correct. I got them to do an angiogram. *Seymour had two hematomas.* One giant aneurysm lay at the anterior base of the brain, where the one clot was. We located the other in the temporal lobe area (associated with what we call an AV fistula or arterio-venous fistula). I was able to go into surgery and clip the aneurysms. Seymour made an uneventful recovery (that is, he encountered no problems) and is now five years old and perfectly normal.

I persisted in that investigation because of an in-depth knowledge of where a traumatic hematoma should form. That knowledge also gave me confidence and pushed me to persist, despite the opposition. If I had not persisted, the hematomas would probably have resolved, the boy would have eventually recovered, and then gone home—only to have the hematomas rupture again. If it happened a second time, he might not have been so fortunate.

I do not mean to imply that I was brighter or more perceptive than the other doctors involved. I relate this incident only because it is one example of how my determination for in-depth learning has paid off because, during my first year at Yale University, I committed myself to in-depth learning; in medical school I decided to learn as much about the human body as possible, and, no matter what area of the body we studied, I tried to learn everything I could.

❖   ❖   ❖   ❖

In the acrostic for Think Big,

I = IN-DEPTH LEARNING

In-depth learning means learning as much about a topic as possible—learning for the sake of knowledge and understanding itself as opposed to learning for the sake of passing a test with high grades or trying to impress people.

Having met many smart students who cannot get good grades, I have concluded that in many of these situations it is because they are not learning materials *in depth*. They tend to stop with an overview of the material and say, "Oh, I know all that." They do not learn things in depth because they are patterning their learning after someone else rather than stopping to ask questions such as, "Do I really know this material?" or "How do I learn best?"

All of us learn differently. For example:

- Some have such developed audio skills that they take in information more easily through the ear than the eye.
- Others find that their best learning comes from talking over a topic with someone else. The give-and-take dialogue sharpens their thinking, causes them to reflect, raises questions, and enables them to hear opposing viewpoints.
- Still others do their best learning by the rote system—repetition and drill.
- I have friends who have to actually *do* something—what we now call hands-on learning.

Of course, the best-disciplined learners combine all the methods in some form.

Sometimes I ask students, "How do you learn best? Which method is the most effective for you?" They do not usually know.

If this is true in your case, here are some helps to discover how you learn best:

Remember three things that you have learned really well, such as:

- completing a science experiment
- solving a tricky algebra problem
- having a solid grasp of the Cold War
- playing difficult pieces on the piano

Ask yourself, How did I learn these things? What methods did I use?

Once you have figured out the answer to these two questions, you then understand your primary learning method, at which point you should adapt your learning situation so that you work from your *strengths,* not from your weaknesses.

For example, if you learn well by repetition, you won't try to learn the major bone structure of the body by listening to a lecture. Instead, you would probably use flash cards. If you are a good reader, you may be able to visualize the things you read about.

Rote may be boring to many as a primary learning tool. Still, consider how many people have learned the words to "My Country 'Tis of Thee" or "Amazing Grace" by repeating the song again and again.

My general rule for in-depth learning says: *Start with methods that work for you.* Use those methods for your major learning projects. Then, strengthen your learning skills by using some of the other methods.

❖   ❖   ❖   ❖

When I entered Yale, I had to face two important facts about myself. First, though I could consider myself a smart enough person, I was not quite as smart as I thought I was. Second, I did not know how to do in-depth studying.

My pattern in school had been to put off studying until just before exam time, concentrate heavily for a day or two, then slide through the tests—and forget half of the information afterward.

Someone who told me that he learned best that way also said, "I study best under pressure."

"No," said a third person, "that's the *only* way you learn."

That was the kind of learning I, too, did best, but when I got to Yale and then to medical school, I had to make changes in my learning methods.

After nearly failing chemistry in Yale's pre-med program—a required course to stay in the program—I got serious about learning. *How do I learn best?* I asked myself. Although I did some experimenting and tried several approaches, by the time I entered medical school I had a solid learning program laid out for myself.

When books are opened, we discover that we have wings.

—*Helen Hayes*

Right off, I realized I did my best learning by myself and through reading books. Listening to lectures was far down on my list. During my four years at the University of Michigan Medical School, I cut many lectures so that I could stay in my room and not be disturbed. *And I read constantly and insatiably.*

My reading began with the required material, then I added other books related to the same topic. To get an in-depth view, I wanted more than one writer's perspective. If we were studying the nervous system, I used three different texts—all good, but each with a slightly different emphasis.

Most days I read from six in the morning until eleven at night, using all the texts and related materials I had available. Someone would loan me class notes and pick up my copy of all handouts.

It did not take long before I knew that I was using the right method for me. For one thing, I had a strong sense of inner satisfaction derived from saying to myself, *I know the nervous system. I understand how it works.* Once my academic performance on tests took a sharp 180-degree turn, I knew that I had become an in-depth learner. I insisted on assimilating more than answers to questions that I would be examined on; I wanted to know everything about the subject.

When the question, "What is the hormonal imbalance that one gets with Cushing's Disease?" appeared on a test, not only did I know the required answer, I knew the underlying mechanism of the hormonal imbalance. No professor was likely to ask that on a test at medical school, but I wanted to know everything extant so that I would have a broader understanding of the human body. The harder I studied, the more I sensed that I was going to become a good doctor. No, that's not quite accurate—I wanted to be the best physician I could be. I knew that to give my best I had to try always to be the best.

Later, when I was doing my neurology rotation as a third-year medical student at the University of Michigan, I had a very exacting chief resident on the service. He would frequently ask the medical students and interns questions about the underlying mechanisms of disease processes.

As I have mentioned elsewhere, I did a great deal of reading during the first two years of medical school after I discovered that reading is the method by which I learn the most easily. One of the subjects I learned extensively about is the endocrine system in the body. In particular, I focused on the pituitary gland, which is located at the base of the brain, and its control of endocrine functions in association with the hypothalamus, which is a portion of the brain.

One day we were examining a patient who had Cushing Syndrome (a problem usually associated with the pituitary hypothalamic access). I was the only individual on the service who was able to go into detail about the underlying mechanism of this disease process. How could I do it? Because of my earlier in-depth reading.

The chief resident stared at me, almost as open mouthed as Mr. Jaeck, my science teacher, had been when I talked about the obsidian. Then he smiled and nodded—a long time.

He was so impressed that he spent extra time with me, encouraging me to keep learning. I felt we had a special relationship. "Fine work," he would say. Or he'd smile and say, "Keep it up."

He did much to help me improve my self-image as someone rising in the discipline of the neurological sciences.

Although I have used an example from my own educational background, I have personally observed in a wide spectrum of life that the kind of knowledge that causes others in our environment to take notice of us—and bestow special attention that can further our progress—applies to whatever we do and whoever we are.

For instance, when the really good (and highly successful!) sellers of insurance contact me, they know the company line and can repeat it without blinking. If, however, I put questions to less well-prepared sellers, involving some in-depth understanding, or I raise questions about the facts behind the actuarial tables, they do not know what to say. Instead of admitting ignorance and adding, "I'll find out and get back to you," they make it worse by trying to obfuscate with words, or by shifting to another topic.

This behavior remains similar with computer operators, auto mechanics, medical personnel, or grocery clerks.

Some of these "surface skimmers" of learning were my classmates in high school, college, and medical school, who learned only what they *had* to know to get by. When pressured to learn more, they fell back on the old chestnut of its not being practical knowledge or relevant information.

"I'll never use this stuff anyway," they say with such certainty that I wonder how they know.

Even today, more than twenty years later, I can hear my older brother, Curtis, complain. While he was very good in math, he was not enthusiastic about geometry and geometrical designs. More than once I heard him grumble about his geometry homework because the problems were quite hard and did not seem particularly relevant.

Fortunately, Mother made sure that Curtis persisted, despite his protests. "Know it better than anyone in the class," Mother told him.

Curtis, who never got caught up in peer pressure as I once did, stayed at geometry, earning an A for the semester and learning the course material well—even though he did not agree that it was an accomplishment that would be supremely relevant to his life.

Today Curtis is a successful engineer who designs aircraft brakes for a major engineering firm. His work calls for him to use a wide variety of geometrical formulas and analytical skills. At the time he was learning geometry, Curtis, who later attended the University of Michigan, had no idea that such skills and knowledge would be a requirement to get into his field.

What my brother is doing now is amazing to me. He has a fine engineering background and would be the first to admit that learning is not always easy, not always fun or appealing, but is necessary. Even though Curtis had no idea when he was learning geometry in high school that he would eventually become an engineer, he persisted anyway. He not only learned what the text and the teachers taught but also assimilated additional information so that one day he could pull out his knowledge to help shape his life.

Curtis is an example of what I define as a practitioner of learning something in-depth. Gaining a solid foundation with any learning set before us can be a door to successful careers.

Another important reality is that unless we make an attempt to learn all that we can, we may never find out whether the matter at hand is something in which we have significant talent. We cannot allow ourselves to be prejudiced against a subject, based upon what someone else has said or just upon the difficulty we encounter in learning.

I am reminded of Eric, a fellow high school student. Because he played football, most of us viewed him as Eric, the macho athlete. None of us thought of Eric as being particularly bright. A few of us did notice that he had an aptitude for math (we probably did not phrase it that way). The truth is that Eric had an incredible knack for understanding and enjoying mathematics. If anything involved equations, Eric gravitated toward it. He was not particularly good in other subjects, but he figured out his special area of ability and cultivated it.

Some of the other players on the football team were so busy living the role of the stereotyped "dumb jock" that they sneered at anyone who even hinted at an interest in anything academic. Fortunately for him, Eric did not listen to his peers. If he had, he would never have discovered a significant God-given talent.

The last time I heard of Eric, he had won a math scholarship to a university in Michigan. I don't know what Eric is doing now, but I know that he is not running around an end zone. I expect that he is doing outstanding work in the field in which he has such obvious talent.

We may have to explore a little. We may need to pursue various channels to discover where our own talents lie. We have to reach for in-depth knowledge so that we can be more proficient in our work and our life goals.

❖ ❖ ❖ ❖

Because Johns Hopkins has earned the reputation as a first-class, international, teaching hospital, we frequently see children from all across the United States, Mexico, and Canada, as well as from many parts of the world. Children who come to us from outside the Baltimore area are nearly always those with intensely difficult problems, who have been previously examined and treated by their own physicians. Many of the doctors do excellent work, but their patient's particular illness lies out of their area of expertise, or perhaps they do not have the needed equipment for treatment. They then refer their patients to Hopkins.

Fortunately, I have been able to come up with solutions for many of the referrals I see in the pediatric neurosurgery clinic. I do not for a moment think that this is because I am any smarter than anyone else or sharper than most of those who refer their patients. Rather, it is because we do have advantages at Hopkins because of its being a teaching hospital and a research center current with the latest developments in our field.

Routinely, before patients and their families arrive, Carol James will have thoroughly evaluated the situation, and I will have studied the medical history. On occasion, I consult with others at Hopkins whose professional opinions I respect—those who give their best to their work.

I have often discovered in treating referral patients from France or Utah, that it is mainly a matter of sitting down with the family and listening carefully. As I listen, another part of me recalls similar medical situations that I have been involved in or read about. Each time, I pull from a vast store of knowledge and experience to try to put all the factors together.

In difficult cases, as well as listening intently to the patient and the patient's family, I take the time to assimilate everything by myself. I reflect, then pull out my past learning so that I can come up with a solution.

A part of doing this derives from asking God to give me insight, to help me grasp the important elements and not be distracted by the less significant matters.

I am convinced that in my field—and I suspect this applies to just about every area of human endeavor—I need perspective for each new challenge. By having a solid foundation of knowledge from which to work, I get perspective.

As strongly as I believe in God, I have never said, "God's going to give me all the answers." God guides; God encourages. But I also highly respect the non-biblical saying, "God helps those who help themselves."

God helps us by:

— encouraging us to use our intelligence;
— urging us to take advantage of learning opportunities;
— inspiring us to acquire the necessary skills and knowledge we need to work effectively in whatever area we have chosen as a career.

Remember:

I = IN-DEPTH KNOWLEDGE

IF WE DEVELOP IN-DEPTH KNOWLEDGE,
IT WILL ENABLE US TO GIVE
OUR BEST TO OTHERS
AND HELP TO MAKE A BETTER WORLD.

Fourteen

Caution: God at Work

*More things are wrought by prayer
Than this world dreams of.*

—Tennyson

Code Blue!" yelled the anesthesiologist.

Until that moment, the surgery on Christine's brain had been going well. I had partially removed a tumor that was invading the brain stem of the four-year-old child. With no warning, she went into cardiac arrest.

Suddenly, whirling activity enlivened the operating room. We had to establish an airway either by mouth-to-mouth resuscitation or by placing a breathing tube down her windpipe.

Someone had to insure circulation again. Often this means giving an electrical shock to the chest wall in an attempt to reestablish a normal cardiac rhythm. With no time to waste, we put clips on her skin. We usually give numerous drugs to aid the heart's beating capacity and to help neutralize chemical imbalances in the blood caused by the arrest.

Oh no, I thought. *We're going to lose her.*

Within the next few seconds—although it seemed much longer —panic seeped through the sterile room. One of the nurses made a call over the intercom for more anesthesiologists.

As my hands moved quickly, I was silently praying, *Lord, I don't know what's going on or what caused this. Fix it, God, please.*

Then my hands firmly gripped Christine's frail body. I had to turn her over to pump her chest (which couldn't be done from the back without injuring her spine). I paused momentarily before I flipped her over. In that instant, her heart started back up again.

"Thank you, Lord," I said aloud. "I don't know what happened, but clearly You fixed it." We were able to proceed without any further difficulty.

We never did figure out what had happened; perhaps it does not matter. What does matter is: I am convinced that God heard my prayer and intervened for young Christine. This is not to say that I count on pulling off a miracle every time something goes wrong. I follow the simple principle that

---

God cares about every area of our lives,
and God wants us to ask for help.

It is imperative to call on God to intervene in our life, especially when we reach the point where we ourselves have become helpless. Because I realize the importance of God in my own life, I decided to make the final letter in the acrostic for Think Big:

G = GOD

Even though G is the last letter, it is certainly not the least important.

Of course, there is another side of this. Some do not feel any need for God—perhaps because they feel so proud of themselves and their abilities that they think they need nothing else.

I recall that during my residency one of the surgeons had an extremely pretentious opinion of his abilities. Also, many of the nonsurgeons believed him to be the only one capable of performing certain types of procedures without significant complications.

His self-inflated attitude seemed to say, "People cater to me and honor me." When everything was not done exactly the way he had envisioned it, he erupted in anger.

By the time he left the operating room, the scrub nurse and

circulators would often be shaking or in tears. He seemed to delight in terrorizing residents as if that were the best way for them to learn.

As I became more experienced, I learned that the operations that he was performing could easily be duplicated by other individuals, with just as low (if not lower) morbidity and mortality —and at a much faster pace.

As I think back on it, I believe that some of his behavior stemmed from his sense of insecurity about his own abilities and self-worth. Generally, I note that the more confident of their abilities that persons are, the less they feel compelled to tell others of their achievements.

I need that kind of self-confidence to deal with the professional jealousy inherent whenever someone achieves the publicity that I have received at such an early age in a field like neurosurgery.

It does not matter what you are doing in a field like this, if you achieve fame, some people invariably come along and accuse you of stealing their patients, of being hungry for publicity, or even of being a charlatan. I have received only one nasty letter from a colleague, but a few friends have heard unkind and harsh comments about me from other colleagues.

At some time in our lives all of us have felt the sting of undeserved criticism—the point at which we can then say, "God, I am doing my best. Give me peace." And God *is* always there with us.

Fortunately, I have received far more positive and encouraging letters from colleagues than negative ones. It seems that the people who are confident and comfortable with what they are doing are pleased to see my success, whereas those who are on shaky ground tend to be jaundiced. Because I believe that what I am doing is for the betterment of our society as well as for the benefit of my patients, I do not become particularly bothered by negative comments.

When some people begin to experience a degree of success, they become overly confident of their own abilities. They behave as if no one else in the world can do what they do. That is to say, they get an exaggerated sense of their own importance and are puffed up with pride, making it difficult for most people to work with them.

These swollen-headed types also usually cease learning. Why shouldn't they? Don't they already know everything in their field (or assume they do)? Despite their talent, they lose their usefulness. They tend to do little but think about themselves. Instead of singing the hymn "How Great Thou Art," their words sound like "How Great I Am."

I wonder if Solomon battled pride and self-aggrandizement because of his brilliance. Perhaps that is one of the reasons he speaks so much in Proverbs against being proud, warning us against getting puffed up:

> Pride goes before destruction, and a haughty spirit
> before a fall (16:18 RSV).

> When pride comes, then comes disgrace; but with
> the humble is wisdom (11:2 RSV).

> A man's pride will bring him low, but he who is
> lowly in spirit will obtain honor (29:23 RSV).

> Haughty eyes and a proud heart, the lamp of the
> wicked, are sin (21:4 RSV).

In contrast, Proverbs speaks often about humility and warns us not to overestimate ourselves. Humility is not groveling and telling everyone how worthless we are—humility is knowing who we are and what God is doing and has done in our lives.

I have worked out a simple formula for humility.

IF WE RECOGNIZE THAT:

1. God created this universe, including us, and

2. God shows that He is much more powerful than we are by what He does and has done in our world, and
3. God gives each of us abilities that we cannot supply to ourselves or explain our worthiness of,

THEN WE ARE HUMBLED.

This basic understanding of who we are in relationship to God enables us to keep perspective. If we grasp that God is both a powerful and a loving force in the world, we become more considerate of others. We comprehend that we must treat other human beings the way we want to be treated. When I meet humble people, I equate their humility with godliness.

In my life I have met and been impressed by a number of godly individuals. Meet three well-known individuals who come to my mind as representative of a godly attitude.

1. *Wintley Phipps*

High on my list is Wintley Phipps, the gospel singer who sang at the conclusion of the last two Democratic national conventions. With his deep, melodious bass voice, Wintley has appeared on many TV programs and is highly respected by other musicians. For instance, he has sung at weddings of famous people like Diana Ross. A person who can make large amounts of money with his enormous talents, he says, "Money is not first in my life. God is first, and I'll never compromise my principles."

Wintley has proved this many times by the type of music he selects, singing only those songs he considers to be true to his principles. Most of the money he has made from his gospel recordings gets channeled back into the church. With proceeds from his records and concerts, for example, Wintley helped restore a famous but dilapidated church in the Washington, D.C. area.

Despite all the things I had heard about him, the real impact of his life registered when I talked with him in person. Just being with Wintley Phipps made me aware that he is constantly thinking about his relationship with God.

2. George Vandeman

Another outstanding individual who has impressed me because of his closeness to God is George Vandeman. For more than forty years, George has preached on radio and TV on a program called *It Is Written*. His broadcast is seen not only everywhere in this country but throughout Europe, and was beamed at the Eastern Bloc nations long before *glastnost*. He is now being heard in China.

Yet, with all his accomplishments—and they are many—he is still a humble man. Because George knows where his ability comes from, he does everything quietly and without fanfare. He is softspoken, practical, nonjudgmental, and one of the nicest guys I have ever met.

3. Robert Schuller

The third celebrity that I have been impressed by is Robert Schuller, who invited me to speak at the Crystal Cathedral on Father's Day in 1989. Schuller, well-known because of TV and his best-selling books, is truly friendly and down-to-earth, and seems to have time for everybody.

In conversing with Dr. Schuller, it became clear to me that he and I share common philosophies about our innate abilities to achieve through positive thinking. Some have latched on to statements that Dr. Schuller has made, and garbled them so that it seems as though he is saying that unless people are high achievers, they are not important. He really means, and I affirm it, that *all of us are valuable because God created us.* Our responsibility is to fulfill whatever potential we have, regardless of where it leads us in life.

Why not be a superb custodian? A first-rate preparer of hamburgers for a fast-food place?

❖   ❖   ❖   ❖

God is important in my life. Part of this, of course, came about because my mother faithfully took me to church. Church was not an option but part of the way of life of our family. It remains that way.

While growing up, I did not have very many adult men to model myself after, my parents having separated when I was only eight. Thus, the heroes of the Bible became my heroes in childhood, as well as my role models. I learned about Jesus Christ who gave Himself for other people, feeling their hurt, and caring about their pain.

I used to think often about Daniel and the three Hebrew boys who believed in God and stayed with their principles—even when the king tried to put them to death.

The hero I related to most is Joseph in the Old Testament. Maybe I identified with him because he had to face the world without his family. I used to mull over his being alone and in prison in Egypt because his jealous brothers had sold him into slavery.

Somewhere during my childhood, and I am sure it was after I started to achieve in school, I sincerely believed that God was capable of taking any person from any circumstances and doing something with that life. Joseph started in slavery but eventually became prime minister of Egypt. Not a bad role model, was he?

It does not matter where we come from or what we look like. If we recognize our abilities, and are willing to learn and to use what we know in helping others, we will always have a place in the world.

I start out each morning with prayer and reading from the Bible, mostly in Proverbs. I pray and read Proverbs each evening. During the course of the day, I frequently ask the Lord to give me wisdom to use the knowledge that I have and to give me perspec-tive and understanding, particularly when difficult situations arise.

God not only gives me those things, but along with them, a confidence that what I am doing is right. That confidence is contagious.

❖   ❖   ❖   ❖

I want to relate the story of Matthew Thompson from Estes Park, Colorado. At age eleven he was diagnosed as having a choroid plexus carcinoma, an extremely rare type of brain tumor. Because it was too vascular, surgeons were able to remove only enough for a biopsy. Matthew then began his struggle to overcome paralysis on one side of his body, as well as an overabundance of other neurological problems. Subsequently, they treated Matt with radiation and chemotherapy. Like others who are aware that their malignant tumors still exist, he faced the uncertainty of life. A year was the most he was expected to survive.

Yet Matt surprised the experts. For nine years, Matt battled his illness. More than once his doctors told him there was nothing more to do. "Just watch," one of them said. "Monitor the tumor. Further surgery will only spread the cancer or cause brain damage."

At one point, the family traveled to Greece for special anti-cancer treatments not obtainable in the United States. For a time, he improved.

In early 1990, the tumor started to grow again. Because of the difficulty with the tumor at the time of the previous surgery, his doctors were reluctant to tackle it surgically. The family began to seek opinions across the country. That is when they contacted our office and talked to Carol James. They subsequently sent us Matt's X-rays and medical records.

The other physicians concluded that the tumor was malignant, not likely to be resectable (cut out), and in a location that would be very difficult to reach. After studying the X-rays carefully, I saw a chance for Matt. I showed the X-rays to Don Long. "I think there is a good chance we can use the track left by the previous surgery to get to the tumor."

Don confirmed that opinion. By using a microscopic technique and lasers, I felt a fair degree of certainty that we could actually remove the lesion.

Furthermore, I felt there was a chance that the original diagnosis had been incorrect. Matt had survived for eight years, which would have been unlikely with that rare type of carcinoma. Matt Thompson was now nineteen years old.

Over the telephone, I explained to his parents, Curt and Pat Thompson. "Yes, I feel that it would indeed be possible to attack this tumor surgically. I also believe there is an excellent chance that we can remove it."

"And what about—about afterward?"

"I think that he could potentially survive with a minimal neurological deficit."

"You mean cured? Normal?" asked Curt.

"I cannot make that promise, but there is a good chance of Matt's living a normal life." These people had had their lives shattered several times by believing that Matt had been cured, only to have the tumor return. After their trip to Greece, they had been sure that Matt was totally cured. Now the tumor had started growing again.

"Oh, thank you," Pat Thompson said. "After hearing so many predictions of how bad—"

"If there is a good chance," Curt Thompson said, "we want you to try. God will help."

The Thompsons were devout Christians and prayed fervently about the situation. "We believe that God has led us to Baltimore," Pat said, "and directly to you for this operation."

In the surgery, which turned out to be exceedingly difficult and took eight or nine hours, we were able to remove the tumor. Matt began to recover.

He subsequently developed numerous complications, including meningitis, tremors, fevers, disorientation, hallucinations, and instability of blood pressure and pulse. Multiple medical consultations were unable to clarify the reason for his deterioration. Eventually, the medical opinion was that he would die.

This was doubly tragic because we had all been so elated initially at being able to remove the tumor. I prayed for a solution to his problem, since we were unable to figure out what was going on. No enlightenment came.

One weekend just as I was about to leave town, I had a strong feeling that Matt would not be alive when I returned. Suddenly, I remembered that thirteen years earlier I had seen a similar situation arise in an elderly man whose prostate had been removed. This man lacked steroids in his system and had reacted very much the same way that Matt was responding some three weeks after surgery.

Immediately I ordered a large dose of steroids for Matt, with a running dose through the weekend. When I returned from my trip, Matt looked like a new person. He was actually sitting up in bed and chatting with his parents. He went on to make an excellent recovery.

More than a year after the surgery, Matt is back at work and has a new lease on life. Had I been concerned about bruising other neurosurgeons' egos, the risk of failure, or had I not asked God for guidance (I believe God helped me remember the case of the elderly man some thirteen years earlier), Matt's outcome would have been considerably different. In my mind there is no doubt that when we go into a situation with confidence, we have a much greater likelihood of being successful and achieving our objectives.

If a baseball player stands at the plate and says, "That pitcher always strikes me out—I don't really have a chance," it is not likely he'll hit a home run. But if he says to himself, "I can hit this guy's pitches, no matter what he throws," he's much more apt to do just that.

❖   ❖   ❖   ❖

About my faith in God, I want to express a few heartfelt thoughts that may sound simplistic or irreverent. As I continue to develop my relationship with Him, I have discovered that God is a nice guy.

I confess that while growing up, I had bought into the concept of God as a stern individual who busily jots down in a book every mistake we make, so that on Judgment Day He can call us up and point to each one, saying, "Why did you do this? I know you did this," and then divulge to everybody present the unpraiseworthy actions of our lives.

I have slowly matured, and have experienced God's help in many crises. I have come to realize that God does not want to punish us but, rather, to *fulfill* our lives. God created us, loves us, and wants to help us to realize our potential so that we can be useful to others.

The relationship that God wants with me became particularly clear to me after Candy and I had children of our own. I realized how much I love my sons and how much I want for them. Of course I want them to be successful, and want to give them everything I can to make them happy. And I realize that God loves me even more than I love my own children.

I cannot give my children everything, but I try to arrange their environment so that they can learn to stand on their own feet, to respect others, and to become valuable citizens.

If I lavish everything on them, they will never reach those goals, but as long as my children know that I love them—that I will stand behind them and do everything within my power to assure their success in life, I feel that I have done what I can for them. They will develop confidence in my love for them, and will know that I only want good for them.

As I have considered my relationship with my sons, it makes it clear to me the relationship that God wants with me and with all the children He has created in the world.

When we rely on our relationship with God, it also makes us more capable individuals. I advocate living by a simple philosophy: *Do your best and let God do the rest.*

❖   ❖   ❖   ❖

Let me share two more incidents. Once when I was operating deep inside a brain, an artery broke loose in an area that I couldn't see. This resulted in vigorous bleeding. Because we couldn't see where the blood was coming from, it looked as though we might lose the patient. Without consciously deciding to do so, I just started praying for God's help. I have learned to act on intuition in such emergencies.

Just then I did something that, in the telling, seems almost irrational. I placed the bipolar forceps into the pool of blood where the bleeding might be coming from. It started sucking away the blood. I pleaded, "God, You've got to stop this bleeding. Please, God, I cannot control it."

Strange as it may seem, at that instant the bleeding stopped without my ever being able to locate its cause. Afterward, the patient awakened and recovered fully.

At another time we had a man from Bermuda who had trigeminal neuralgia (an extremely painful condition of the face caused by irritation of the fifth cranial nerve). Before we had methods to treat this condition, many patients committed suicide because of the constant pain.

I had to put the needle into an exceptionally small hole at the base of his skull and pass it up to the level of the ganglion. This process requires a skill in which I had developed a great deal of proficiency during my days as a medical student. On that particular day, however, no matter what I did, I could not get the needle into the hole. I had worked at this for nearly two hours before it occurred to me that perhaps I should give up.

Just before quitting, I finally prayed, *Lord, I cannot get the needle in. There is no way I can do it. I am going to take this needle and push it one more time. I want You to guide it into the hole, because I cannot seem to do it.*

I took the needle, pushed it, and it went right through the hole as if it had a mind of its own. A feeling of deep gratitude came over me.

I feel that it is a little risky to relate an incident like this because I can almost hear skeptics say, "Oh, come on, Ben, that is ridiculous. Why would you even say a thing like that?"

Yet, for me it is not absurd; it is what I expect. In talking with other Christian surgeons, I have learned that some of them understand because they have experienced similar feelings of God guiding their hands.

When we develop a relationship with God and believe that He is working through us, we still have moments of helplessness—when God has an opportunity to do something for us. This happens when we give our best—which, at the particular moment, does not seem good enough. Ready to give up, we say aloud or silently, "I cannot do any more, Lord. I need *You.*"

At such moments we provide God with the opportunity to respond. Truly, "Man's extremity is God's opportunity."

G = GOD

IF WE ACKNOWLEDGE OUR NEED FOR GOD, HE WILL HELP US.

Fifteen

Reaching for Success

*Self-love, my liege, is not so vile a sin as
self-neglecting.*
—Shakespeare

M*arian was a highly* accomplished violinist and quite proficient on both the piano and organ. She came to us, diagnosed as having a severe facial pain syndrome. We thought we found a lesion at one area of the skull. Although it was in a difficult location to reach, we decided that was probably the cause of her pain. Don Long and I operated on her together.

In the post-operative period, Marian developed marked swelling in her right temporal lobe (on the right side of her brain)—an area heavily associated with artistic ability. The swelling extended into the parietal lobe (also heavily involved with musical ability).

That same night, I had to go back in and do a temporal lobectomy—an operation in which part or all of the temporal lobe of the brain has to be removed. Not knowing whether or not she would survive, Marian's situation concerned me deeply.

Once we realized that she was going to live, we breathed more easily. My next concern revolved around her speech and motor functions. Gradually she regained them.

She progressed so well that only one area of concern remained —her musical ability. Because we had taken out part of the right side of her brain, Don Long and I asked each other, "Will it impair her musical ability?" All the evidence indicated that she would no longer have significant musical skills.

"I understand," said Bob, her husband, when he heard our prognosis about her musical impairment. Bob is a pastor, and the whole family is very devout. They prayed constantly for Marian's improvement. "We've been praying about this," he said as he touched his wife's hand and smiled at her. "We are both convinced that she will eventually regain all her abilities—including her musical ability."

I had given them my medical opinion and did not say much more. Certainly never wanting to take hope away from anyone, I really did not know what to say.

As we continued to talk, I remember Bob's saying, "Ben, if the Lord wants that musical ability to be there, it really does not matter what has to be taken out to save her life. It will still be there."

Marian went home shortly afterward. After several months of rehabilitation, to my surprise, Marian once again returned to her music. Not only did she regain her excellent ability with the violin, but she was able to play the piano and organ as well as she had before. To make the miracle even more remarkable, her pain had gone away, too.

Marian's story is reminiscent of the story of Beth, the little girl from Connecticut. In 1987, Beth underwent a hemispherectomy (removal of half her brain because of intractable seizures). If the surgery had not been done, she would eventually have died or been institutionalized. Because we had removed the left hemisphere of Beth's brain, we worried that her mathematical ability had been impaired.

"We'll just have to wait and see," I told her parents.

"She is alive and well," her mother said. "That is more than we expected when we brought her here."

The last I heard from the family, three years after surgery, was that Beth had become number one in math in her class.

The preceding cases outline two successful surgeries and two successful recoveries—both of them against medical odds, for which I was elated and thankful. But for me, success did not start with the positive outcomes after surgery. For me, success began very early when, at the junior high level, my schoolwork had turned things around academically, and I began to realize that within my grasp lay the ability to extricate myself from a poverty-stricken environment. I had confidence in my ability to do just about anything I wanted to do with my life. Since from the age of eight I had not wanted to be anything but a doctor, I therefore expected to be a *successful* doctor.

In those days, Mother sometimes drove Curtis and me to Bloomfield Hills and Grosse Pointe, Michigan, to the section where many affluent people lived. As we passed the estates, I used to say, "Someday I am going to live in a house like that. I am going to have a nice car, and go on a nice vacation, and have a nice job and a nice title. I know that is going to happen."

Those words did not come out as a vague wish or as if I had set my jaw with determination—I spoke from a sense of assurance and deep conviction. Mother had taught us, and I sincerely believed in, the so-called American dream. I still do.

By the time I was thirteen, I was convinced that we can take charge of our own lives—that *we do not have to be victims of circumstance.*

Although I expected to be successful, I had no idea that I would ever become a director of pediatric neurosurgery at a major teaching hospital. I had no idea that I would be thrust into the limelight to the degree that I have been. To have the opportunities to exert influence in so many different areas simply did not occur to me. Nor did it ever come to my mind that my success would be involved with innovative surgery. That, quite frankly, was the part that God arranged.

God convinced me to stay in academic medicine (that is, on the staff of a teaching hospital). For a long time I had assumed that I would ultimately go into private practice, but when all the extraordinary cases started coming my way, and I saw opportunities to push ahead in my field, I began to think about remaining at Hopkins. I have been extremely happy in my work.

In the midst of this I want to say that God has made things work out successfully for me by giving me the talent to be a surgeon —the ability to think and operate in three-dimensional terms.

As I have moved up the American ladder of success, my gratitude to God has deepened. By telling my own life story about a boy from a broken home, in a poverty-stricken environment, with poor grades and a bad attitude—and emphasizing that God has enabled me to do the things I yearned to accomplish—I also have had the opportunity to show people that God is still active today.

Remaining a victim of circumstance is a state of being that we choose, a choice that

> — allows us to blame other people
> — lets us blame circumstances
> — permits us to avoid responsibility for our lives
> — encourages us to feel sorry for ourselves, and
> — guarantees that we will stay victims.

No one has to be a victim!

In writing *Think Big,* I want to discuss the concept of success —which the word for, unfortunately, has often been mistakenly used. For some, success means making it to the top of the ladder, regardless of what one has to do to get there. These same people measure success by what they accumulate and how many millions of dollars they are worth.

Frankly, it saddens me when I speak at schools and during the question-and-answer period students ask:

— "What kind of house do you live in?"
— "How many cars do you have?"
— "Do you have a swimming pool?"

As far as I am concerned, the money and what it buys are insignificant. Achievers are going to have those things anyway. What *is* important—what I consider success—is that we make a contribution to our world.

To some, success in life means putting more into life than we take out. I think of success *as reaching beyond ourselves and helping other people in specific ways.* This can be as simple as being a father who inspires his children to make the best of their lives—being a mother who guides her children toward faith in God and confidence in themselves—or being faithful to whatever enterprise one undertakes and doing it with a determination to be the best at that task.

I like the words of Paul in writing to the Colossians. He told wives, husbands, children, fathers, and slaves how to live and do their best for each other, summing it up with these words: "And whatever you do, whether in word or deed, do it all in the name of the Lord Jesus, giving thanks to God the Father through him" (3:17).

In our society more women than ever are moving into the work force. Some now look down on those who stay home for their husbands and children. Because of the positive influence of my mother, I am doubly pleased that Candy is enjoying her success right now as a wife and as a mother. When our three sons become adults, I hope they will be able to look back at my positive influence and especially the influence of their mother, who spends much more time than I with them.

I know personally the tremendous influence that a mother can exert. Although I am forty, I still remember comments my own mother made to me. Remarkably consistent, not only did Mother give us the same message any number of times, but she found a variety of ways to express it. And, whether we liked to admit it or not, what she said did make sense.

I can think of so many ways that she would push us to learn the things that would help us most. Often she would pick up a textbook and ask, "What edition is that?"

I would examine it and say perhaps, "The third."

"Know what that means, Bennie? That means the writers made improvements. They gained more knowledge, so they added it to the book. Why don't you read it critically? Maybe you'll write the next edition yourself."

Her all-time favorite, of course, was "If anybody can do something you can do it—except you can do it better." She said that so many times that I came to believe I was supposed to do *everything* at least as well as anybody else who had tried to do it. Later, we understood that Mother did not mean that Curtis and I had to be number one in everything—she just wanted us to give our best to whatever tasks we had to do.

"There is absolutely no reason not to do your best," she said.

Many times, I would learn that when I did my best and stayed at it, I did not always turn out to be number one. "Some folks may be smarter, but they won't work as hard," she'd say. "If you give your best, you cannot lose."

Some other ideas about success that Mother ingrained in us in our growing-up years, that I not only learned but obviously have never forgotten are:

As long as you are satisfied that you've done your best, then that is all you have to do.

The best way to please yourself is to know you've done the best for yourself that you can do.

Clothing is not important. Houses, cars, and bank accounts—none of those things are important. You know what is important? Knowledge and hard work—the abilities that allow you to acquire those things.

You want to know what's important? Here is how you figure it out. Just let someone take all the things away from you like money, cars, and houses. They can take them, but you can get them back if you have the appropriate knowledge and learn to use it. But if someone takes away your knowledge and your willingness to give your best, you've automatically lost everything that is important—and you won't get them back.

Mother had bits of advice about the friends with whom I spent my time. Often I did not like what she said, but she was usually right.

"Bennie, look closely at that boy. Is that what you want to be like?" she asked me about one of my friends who cut school and continually got into trouble in the neighborhood.

"No," I said, "but I am just being a friend."

"You become like the people you spend your time with. You have to be careful in selecting friends. Sometimes people think they can hang out with a certain crowd and are sure they won't become like them. They think that somehow they are immune from the influence. But they're only fooling themselves. After a while they begin to act like them and absorb aspects of their personality without even noticing it. Before long they start becoming the same kind of individuals as those they hang out with."

That is one lesson that I learned the hard way in high school. For most of the tenth grade, my friends were the kind who only wanted to play and to wear fancy clothes. The more time I spent with them, the more I wanted to be like them. It was a hard year for me, but I learned about the way other people influence us.

Today I advise listeners: "Associate with the people you want to be like. It does not matter whether we are students, or middle-aged, or elderly. *We are still able to grow as long as we are alive.*" If we want a successful life—a life of inner peace and of content-ment—we have to work for it. Can we find a better way to make it happen than by being around those we want to be like? This also keeps us away from the harmful element who know they are losers and will not do anything to change.

Nonachievers in this world put great effort into helping others fail. They cajole, sneer, criticize, and argue. In school they can produce a long list of names to call fellow students, such as "teacher's pet," "nerd," and "egghead."

When kids who are the targets of such ridicule tell me about their distress, I suggest that they answer their critics this way: "Let's see what I am doing in twenty years and compare it with what you are doing. Then we'll know who made the right choice."

That is how I handled it when I left my disruptive group in tenth grade. Two years later, they were part of the class who voted me the person "most likely to succeed." Perhaps they did not like what I did, but I suspect that they may have envied me a little and perhaps wished that they had done likewise.

Not only did Curtis and I get constant criticism at school, but parents in our neighborhood treated Mother badly. "Don't you realize what you are doing to those boys?" I heard one mother say.

"Sure, I know. I am raising them right."

"Raising them right, huh! They're going to hate you when they grow up because you are so strict and mean."

"They can hate me all they want," Mother said, "but they're going to be successful first!"

In this way my mother talked to us and to others.

❖   ❖   ❖   ❖

Some people complain about injustice in our society. They cannot be successful because everything is stacked up against them. Frequently I have heard individuals say that they have to be twice as good as anyone else to get equal breaks. Because of their ethnicity, language, or socio-economic background, they feel that if they do not do things twice as well as the majority of the population, they will not receive equal opportunities.

Whether this is true or not is not the real issue. I believe that *God expects us to do our best at everything* we undertake. If we always do our best and trust in the Lord's guidance, we automatically conduct our affairs better than most other individuals who do not have the same mindset.

We do not have to compare our achievements with those of others. We need only to ask ourselves one question: Have I given my best?

Having read these chapters about Thinking Big, put them into practice. Recall each letter in the acrostic to remind yourself that *you* can Think Big.

❖ ❖ ❖ ❖

By Thinking Big, we can transform our world.

T = TALENT
If we recognize our talents, use them appropriately, and choose a field that uses those talents, we will rise to the top of our field.

H = HONESTY
If we live by the rule of honesty and accept our problems, we can go far down the road of achievement.

I = INSIGHT
If we observe and reflect and commit ourselves to giving our best, we will come out on top.

N = NICE
If we are nice to others, others respond to us in the same way—and we can give our best for each other.

K = KNOWLEDGE
If we make every attempt to increase our knowledge in order to use for human good, it will make a difference in us and in our world.

B = BOOKS
If we commit ourselves to reading, thus increasing our knowledge, only God limits how far we can go in this world.

I = IN-DEPTH KNOWLEDGE
If we develop in-depth knowledge, it will enable us to give our best to others and help to make a better world.

G = GOD
If we acknowledge our need for God, He will help us.